Please Don't Leave Me

Please Don't Leave Me

The heartbreaking journey of one man and his dog

Michelle Clark
with Joe and Ann Cusack

SEVEN DIALS

First published in the United Kingdom in 2023 by Seven Dials,
an imprint of The Orion Publishing Group Ltd
Carmelite House, 50 Victoria Embankment,
London EC4Y 0DZ

An Hachette UK company

1 3 5 7 9 10 8 6 4 2

A CIP catalogue record for this book is
available from the British Library.

ISBN (Paperback): 978 1 409 19545 0
ISBN (eBook): 978 1 409 19546 7

Typeset by Born Group

Printed and bound in Great Britain by Clays Ltd, Elcograf S.p.A.

www.orionbooks.co.uk

To my beautiful children, Bradley & Eloise,
and to my many homeless friends with
Dogs On The Streets.

Prologue

Painfully thin and gaunt, he looked at me longingly as I watched from the top of the ward. The sound of bleeps and the whir of machines reverberated in the background against the general hubbub of visiting time. People were coming and going. Smiling friends and reassuring families, kindness and concern etched on their faces, were packed in tight, huddled into the cramped dormitories that ran off the main corridor. Looking around, it was hard not to be moved by the tell-tale bald heads, pallid skin tones and missing eyelashes as patients lay helpless in their beds, hooked up to state-of-the-art, hi-tech monitors, syringe drivers and drip lines. Children excitedly raised and lowered the remote-control beds, laughing as they emptied the hand sanitisers while scoffing chocolates and treats brought in for their desperately sick relatives.

Mustering a smile as he saw me walk onto the ward, Arthur Dumbliauskas battled to hoist his tired body up in the bed, wincing in pain as he did so. The bright summer sun shone through the light blue, washed-out NHS curtain that barely covered the edges of the window.

'Hello, Arthur.' I smiled as I handed him a bar of his favourite Galaxy chocolate and a bunch of grapes. 'How are you feeling today?'

'Oh, Michelle,' he said. 'I'm so worried about Kaizer. How is he? Is he OK? He frets when we're apart.'

'He's fine, Arthur. I handed him my iPhone, a freshly taken photo of Kaizer on the screen.

I had only known Arthur for a short time, but already we had connected; I felt as though I'd known him all my life. While I found myself worrying about him, I knew he was in the right place – and so too was his best friend and life companion, his beautiful Staffie-Ridgeback cross, Kaizer, who was safe and sound in the Dogs on the Streets kennels. A tear trickled from Arthur's sad brown eyes. His craggy skin was weathered from years of rough sleeping, and his earlobes drooped under the weight of his piercings, but he was clean, well cared for, and had everything he needed – for the time being, at least.

'I've got nobody on my side,' he muttered through his tears. 'Nobody to love and nobody to care for, except Kaizer.'

'I'm on your side, Arthur,' I told him, taking hold of his hand. It was coarse and roughened from countless years spent outside in merciless winds. 'And I'm going nowhere.'

'Will you come with me to speak to the doctor?' he said in his fading Eastern European accent.

'Of course I will,' I told him. With my hand resting supportively on his shoulder, I walked by his side as the porters pushed him in a wheelchair past the legions of loving families. I smiled and whispered, 'Don't worry, Arthur, everything will be all right; I'm right here by your side.'

I could sense the fear oozing from him. He was over a thousand miles from anything that could remotely be thought of as a home, in a foreign country without his family, without his mother, without his children and without the familiar faces and things that comfort us in times of trouble. He'd spent years drifting through the unforgiving streets of London. Expressionless faces passing him, with the occasional kind soul buying him a cup of tea and a sandwich or dropping a few quid into a paper cup placed on the pavement in front of him and his faithful dog. Of course, Arthur was just one of the countless thousands who lose themselves and end up on the streets with nothing. But there was something different about him. Something that inspired me.

The consultant didn't even look up from behind her desk as I sat down with Arthur in his hospital-issue wheelchair. I could see he was nervous as he clasped one hand around a clenched fist and looked to me for support.

'Right, Arthur, I'm sorry to have to tell you this,' she said, looking up from her papers and tapping on a computer keyboard. 'Your test results are back, and I'm afraid to say that your cancer is in an advanced stage, and you have no more than six months to live.'

'My God,' I bellowed in sheer outrage. 'This is not on. You can't just drop a bombshell like that without even making proper eye contact. This is outrageous. He is a human being with feelings and people who love him. Show him the dignity that he bloody well deserves, you callous sod.'

With her wiry grey hair and thick-rimmed tortoiseshell glasses, she looked for all the world like a junior admin clerk processing an everyday task, an attitude born of years of repeatedly dishing out life-changing news to the unsuspecting masses. She looked down at Arthur and, like so much of society, saw him as the living embodiment of the 'great unwashed'.

'Madam,' she said to me. 'You will have to compose yourself or I will have to ask you to leave the room.'

'Do whatever you want to me,' I screamed. 'But you will show my friend some respect. And it is Mr Dumbliauskas to you, if you don't mind.'

She looked aghast, offended, affronted; outrage etched on her face.

'And can I ask who you are?' she demanded authoritatively. 'What is your interest in this?'

Arthur looked at me. He was devastated; he had just had the news that his days were numbered. But a serene calmness had come over him and in that tiny instant, he had changed. It was almost as if the pain he'd carried around for all these years had suddenly been taken away. The consultant had told him that he was going to die, but for Arthur, this news seemed to have brought a sense of relief that washed away the anguish of feeling unwanted.

'She is my true family,' Arthur spoke up, almost majestically. 'Michelle is my next of kin.'

My heart melted as he bravely spoke up for himself. I was filled with an intense pride in his courage and compassion for this lovely, humane man.

'Mr Dumbliauskas,' the doctor said, clearing her throat. 'We need to start your chemotherapy straight away. If I can just ask you to sign here . . .'

But as the consultant passed Arthur the consent letter to sign, he pushed it away.

'I don't want any of your treatments.' He smiled passively. 'I just want to see my dog and live out my last days with him.'

Outside in the corridor, Arthur stopped his chair, and as I stooped down to his eye level, he asked, 'Is that OK with you, Michelle?'

'Yes,' I told him, holding back the tears. 'Yes, of course. I promise you I will fight your corner, and I will make damn sure that you live out your days with your best friend.'

'You really are my angel,' he said with a bright smile.

CHAPTER 1

Pop-Up Fun at the Fair

The dark places in which I found myself throughout my teenage years felt like they would engulf me at times. I just could not see a way out. Even though, looking back, I was probably being a moody teenager, I felt a real sense of unhappiness most of the time back then. I would often take solace in our family cat, Pimms. He was so cool, so distant and, well, cat-like! That's the thing about cats – you know them and love them, but everything has to be on their terms, and that's just the way it is. They don't seem to really need anybody – except, of course, for my mum, who fed him every day!

'Go on, Mum,' I'd say to her as she stood in our kitchen cooking the tea. 'Tell me the story about how you came to call him Pimms.'

With a wry smile, she would start all her tales with her trademark, 'Well, it was like this, Michelle.

'A fella I know came into the local pub one night and pulled a tiny little kitten out of his pocket. He said, "Anyone want a pussy cat?" And just as he put the poor little thing down, the kitten made a beeline for me, knocking a glass of Pimm's all over the table as he did so. On top of that, we were about to move into our new house at Pimms Avenue; the coincidence was astonishing. It was meant to be, so I said "Right, little pussy cat, your time has come. It is Pimms o'clock!"'

Without knowing why, I would roll about laughing as she told me the same story over and over again. That was our beautiful little Pimms: handsome, independent, streetwise Pimms.

I spent a lot of time with our cat, and I loved him dearly. He was my soul mate, my confidante, and he and my family helped me through some very dark times, but I was a teenager and I needed something more. No matter how hard I tried, I just couldn't shake the idea that nobody ever noticed me. It was like I was the invisible girl. Night after night, I would lie on my bed, dreaming about being somewhere else, and wishing I could up sticks, leave and start all over again in a happier and more colourful place. So, when I spotted the trucks and caravans rolling into the local park, it was like a red rag to a bull. The very idea of setting up camp, carrying everything you owned and bringing all the fun with you on the back of a lorry, then disappearing in a flash, appealed to my very core.

'Penny, you'll never guess what.' I stood at my best friend's front door, gabbling excitedly. 'There's a funfair that has set up on Broomhill Park. Are you coming?'

'Really?' she enthused. 'But I haven't got any money, Michelle.'

'Don't worry,' I told her, jangling my pocketful of change. 'I've got a couple of quid. Get your coat and let's get going.'

From a very early age, I was left to my own devices, and if I wanted to get something, I had to earn the money to pay for it. I was up at the crack of dawn and working in a market by the age of eleven. At weekends, I used to clean cars for a pound a time. I worked bloody hard, and some days I washed that many cars, my hands sometimes felt like they were dropping off with the freezing cold, my fingers shrivelled up like turkey claws!

'But Michelle, it's getting late,' Penny said nervously, looking down their hallway towards the living room, where her mum and dad were sitting, drinking tea and watching telly.

'Oh, sod that for a game of soldiers, Penny.' I laughed, taking her by the arm. 'Let's go and have some fun for a change.'

The light was fading; it was getting dark. The traffic noise and the unrelenting city hubbub from the North Circular Road gradually faded away as the muffled beat of loud music took hold. Nesting birds withdrew from the chaos as dusk descended, their quiet shattered by the bright lights and swirling madness coming from behind the dense clump of trees down by the boating lake.

'Come on, it'll be fine,' I told Penny as we skipped along the edge of the road around the park.

'D'you think we'll be OK out here in the park at night?' she worried. 'Maybe we should turn back and go home. We could come back tomorrow afternoon.'

'Oh, don't be a wuss.' I laughed. 'It'll be a giggle.'

Hoisting up our gleaming white rah-rah skirts, Penny and I climbed through a gap in the railings and ran across the fields towards the fun fair that had sprung to life out of nowhere. A park that seemed so harmless and friendly in the calm light of day – a safe environment where people walked their dogs, mums watched over little kids as they played on the swings against the background of whistles from football matches, and dads stood with their sons as they sailed remote-control boats on the lake – took on a very different feel at night. In the hours of darkness, it changed and became a place of danger and excitement: a place where anything was possible, and you never quite knew who or what could be lurking behind the bushes.

As we got nearer, the muffled echo of the music came together, and the disjointed beat fell into place. The air was filled with Andy Williams's 'Can't Take My Eyes Off You' ringing out all around the trees and fields. 'Dah de, dah de de dah de dah-dah de-dah,' we sang at the tops of our voices and linked our arms together as we danced towards the fair. 'I love you baby . . .'

The glow of the illuminations peeping over the tree-line and flashing lasers bursting through the branches drew people in from the surrounding streets and houses.

Darkened silhouettes approached from all directions, all smiles and laughter, looking for some fun. Penny and I joined the throng, marching arm in arm towards the bright lights, as the music blared and screams echoed from the rides flying around the wide-open spaces.

Everything in sight was on wheels with huge, big oily trucks waiting behind the scenes, ready for the fun to be packed away in readiness for a new park or town. Then the next morning, at the drop of a hat, it would all be gone, disappearing in a flash, with nothing left except a few tyre tracks in the mud and a covering of gravel and sand. I was both fascinated by and drawn to the whole thing, sucked in by the sheer rootlessness and nomadic way of life these wandering souls had. They peddled fun, laughter, excitement and thrills, and I was utterly enthralled.

The smell of axle grease and diesel and the sickly-sweet tang of candy floss filled my nostrils as we got nearer. The grass under our whitened plimsolls turned to woodchip and stones, a temporary surface laid out for the adrenaline-packed, fun-filled week.

We hugged each other and giggled like the naughty schoolgirls we were as we ambled around the stalls and gazed at the rides. A dark-haired lad, with his shirt sleeves rolled up, skipped with a fearless elegance and poise across the rotating and undulating wooden floor of the waltzers. Madonna's 'Like A Virgin' blasted out of the speakers as he leaped fearlessly from one car to the other, pirouetting with a death-defying swagger as he grabbed hold of the back of the brightly coloured cars and span them wildly, smiling and laughing as the people inside screamed at the tops of their voices. Dumbstruck, I stared dreamily at the way he strutted around the spinning cars, inches from harm but without a care in the world.

'Oh my God.' I held my hands to my mouth. 'Take a look at that guy!'

'Wow, he's amazing.' Penny beamed as I pointed him out to her.

'Are you coming on with me, Michelle?' she said.

My eyes lit up. Penny was as excited as me, and I knew she felt the same thrill and exhilaration as I did.

'Yeah!' we blurted out in unison.

Skipping up onto the platform, we dashed ahead of the crowds and plonked ourselves down, pulling the metal safety bar in tight so nobody else could get in with us. My heart was beating nineteen to the dozen as I watched the young guy going from car to car taking money, and chatting and flirting with all the goggle-eyed girls. We sat excitedly, clinging to each other, terrified.

'Hello, my darlings,' he said to us as he pulled down the safety guard.

'Fifty pence each, my lovelies.' He smiled as he took our money. 'Hang on to your hats now; you're in for the ride of your lives.'

Slamming the safety barrier into place, he skipped onto the next car with his tatty leather bag of change hanging around his neck. His cheeky smile was mesmeric as well as infectious, and there was a carefree wildness about him.

We started off slowly, then went faster and faster as the ride span into full throttle. Kajagoogoo's 'Too Shy' played at full blast on the speakers, and I could feel myself sliding up against Penny as the engine roared and the waltzers gathered momentum. Just then, I couldn't help noticing a little dog, a Staffie, sitting quietly at the side of the ride. He looked so cute, and had beautiful big brown eyes. As we came around again, he'd disappeared.

'What's your names, girls?' the young guy asked as he leaped over to our car, holding on to the back of it, poised to launch us.

'Miiiccchhh . . .' I gasped.

Just then, a powerful wind forced my mouth wide open and filled my cheeks. I didn't even have time to say my name before he sent us spinning out of control. My stomach turned upside down as the adrenaline rushed to my heart. Screaming, I grasped the handrail tight with both hands as Penny and I clung on for dear life. The strong smell of burning sugar and the pungent whiff of hot dogs hung thick in the air as we cut through it at breakneck speed. The lights in the canopy above us twisted in a revolving blur as Michael Jackson carried us away into the stratosphere. I was in seventh heaven.

'I've got enough for one more ride and some candy floss to share,' I said to Penny as we stepped off. Walking around the fair, I was captivated by the whole place. Being there, out late at night without any adults to hold us back, we felt free. The rows of stalls were packed with people firing air guns at little pop-up targets, kids with their mums and dads hooking ducks on poles, a macho fella handing a giant purple teddy bear to his blushing girlfriend; it was a magical place. But what intrigued me most of all was the fact that in no time at all, it would all be gone, only to pop up somewhere completely different on the other side of town.

'Hello,' I said to a young lad wearing badly fitting oily blue overalls. 'Do you work here?'

'Er, yes, love.' He smiled, looking at the huge spanner in his hand and standing over a broken dodgem with its bits all over the floor. 'Are you having a good time, girls?' he asked.

'Oh yes,' Penny said. 'It's brilliant.'

'Do you live here, too?' I asked shyly.

'Yes, I live in that caravan over there,' he said. 'Are you from around here? What's your names?'

We told him our names and started chatting. He told us his name was John, and he lived with his dad, also called John. The man on the waltzers, amazingly enough, was called John too! The John we were speaking to had been born on the road and lived his life moving all over the country, and sometimes overseas. I couldn't believe how good that sounded. It all seemed perfect to me.

13

'What about school?' I asked. 'How do you do that?'

'Oh, I don't bother usually.' He laughed. 'I have some lessons from my aunty and the education people are always on our backs. But we don't care; this is who we are, and this is how we live.'

'So, you're like gypsies?' I said.

'No, we're not gypsies as such, but we live on the road like they do, moving from town to town.'

'Why are you all called John?' I laughed.

'Why are you called Michelle and you Penny?'

'Well, that's what our mums and dads chose for us.'

'There's your answer, Michelle.' He laughed.

'So, where are you off to next?' I asked, picking a piece of caramelised candy floss out of my teeth.

'Chingford.' He smiled. 'Well, at least I think we're going to Chingford.'

'Where's Chingford?' Penny asked.

'Out East,' he said. 'Essex way, I think.'

The sugar rush went straight to my head, and I came over all giddy. John Junior told us that they were in the park for the next week, and that he'd get us some free rides if we fancied coming back the following night.

'Let's go on the twister!' Penny said, grabbing my arm.

'Bye, John,' I shouted as we dashed off. 'I've got a feeling we'll meet again soon.'

We ran towards a giant spider-shaped machine. Lightbulbs danced up and down the brightly coloured steel arm of the ride that connected to the two-seater cars at the end. We stood in line, waiting for our turn as we watched the people on the ride before us.

'Georgina!' A large woman with a blonde rinse and set started shouting at the top of her voice. 'Stop the ride! Stop the ride!' Just as she got her words out, the car span towards us, and a spray of sickly foul-smelling liquid splattered all around, missing me and Penny by inches. A blonde girl sitting in the outside of one of the cars had started throwing up as the ride whizzed around. Each time she retched, her vomit sprayed in a perfectly symmetrical, zig-zag pattern all over the place – and even on some of the people standing in the queue.

'Oh my God.' We laughed as we ran to take cover from the projectile puke. 'I reckon she's had a few too many hot dogs and toffee apples!'

We had to wait an extra twenty minutes while the men of the ride cleaned the cars and argued with the blonde-haired woman, as well as various people complaining of getting covered by the content of the girl's stomach. For us, it all added to the fun, and we jumped in a car – making sure it wasn't the one the girl had thrown up in! The wind rushed through our hair as we span with terrific G-force. The car screeched to a halt and lost speed, before changing direction suddenly and whizzing back the other way. I caught glimpses of laughing faces as we raced past.

'That was brilliant!' I gushed.

'Come on, Michelle. I'm for the high jump when I get in,' Penny said as we climbed out of the car. 'It's getting far too late. My mum will kill me.'

'Oh, five more minutes,' I moaned.

'But we haven't got any money left,' she pleaded.

I could see the fear in her face when she realised it was past ten o'clock. It was pitch black and we were both going to be in big trouble when we got home.

Penny and I were like two lost little souls, both on the outside looking in, with different interests and ideas to the rest, and we were always somehow separated from the in-crowd. Like me, she spent most of her time in her bedroom, staring into space and wishing she was somewhere else. Make-up and hair weren't her thing and, like me, she wasn't a fan of the Mod fashion that all the other kids seemed to be into. Most of the other girls where we lived dressed in black-and-white mini dresses and dainty fake Mary Quant strap-over shoes, with tight bobbed hair and severe black eyeliner. The boys wore cheap suits and fishtail parkas, covered in target badges, and dreamed of riding to Brighton on Lambrettas and fighting with greasy bikers, pretending they were just like Sting in *Quadrophenia*. I thought it was all rather pathetic, not my thing at all. But although I laughed at them for getting drunk at their 'Mod-only' parties, sometimes, when I was feeling a bit down, I would think it must be nice to be a part of something, a group sharing similar interests and with a definite sense of belonging. Penny was the only person I could relate to, even if it was in a small way. Day after day we sat in school, listening to the other girls drone on about make-up and boys – I was sick of it. I wanted other things. I had no idea *what*, but I knew I wanted something else.

CHAPTER 2

Out on the Streets

At home, things were not much better. I spent almost all my time in my room by myself. I was a loner, with only my cat, Pimms, to keep me company. Staring at the picture of Limahl from Kajagoogoo that I'd carefully cut out of *Smash Hits* magazine and pinned to my bedroom wall, I dreamed of other things. He was so fantastic, his haircut so 'with it', and their music was incredible. But while I thought I might have actually loved Limahl at one stage, I could now see he was just a pin-up, a make-believe fantasy and a plastic pop star. He wasn't real, and probably wouldn't be half the man he looked and sang like. Right from my early teenage years, I decided firmly that idols were not my thing.

Life was drab and boring; I had no interest at all in slapping on make-up and spending hours doing my hair to make me look old enough to get into the local pubs. I despised the behaviour of the other girls, spending their days in rollers, nicking lippy from their older sisters or their mums, and for what? Drinking lager and lime in a crappy old pub, trying to look big. No, that wasn't for me; I wanted fun and I wanted excitement of a different sort.

To say my desires were a world away from my everyday life would be an understatement; I couldn't shake the thoughts that bothered me. Time and time again, I found myself creeping out of the garden gate and out into the night. Walking along empty roads and avenues, passing houses that all looked the same, I often asked myself why I was so unhappy when the other people living here were not. Our home was in quite an affluent area; there were trees and well-established bushes, nice cars parked in neat driveways belonging to nice, cheerful families, who all had places to go to and things to do. I knew every inch of the place: the cracks in the pavement, the occasional faded paint spill, the street signs, and which way was which. It was all too familiar to me, and I hated it. That terrible feeling of doom hit me in the stomach as I wandered aimlessly underneath the orange sodium glare of the streetlights, crossing the road whenever I saw someone coming my way, avoiding all contact.

'Hold your breath till they've gone, Michelle,' I told myself, fixing my gaze away from the imposing presence of strangers. My anxiety would only subside once they had passed; then I could breathe again.

I wondered what kind of dramas might be happening behind all those closed doors. Already I'd learned that most people, like most situations, are rarely quite how they seem at first. I was no more than twelve or thirteen years old, but I knew I had to get away.

One evening, with no more than a pound or two in my pocket, I jumped on a bus and headed towards the maze of streets of Central London. Timidly, I climbed the stairs to the top deck and wedged myself into the front seat. Though the bus was almost empty, I knew that if I sat in the two front seats directly above the driver, people were far more likely to get to the top of the stairs and walk down the bus rather than sitting next to me, a young girl sitting alone at the front. Behind me, an old man had fallen asleep, his heavy breathing rhythmically merging into the deep rumble of the bus's engine as it trawled through the city at night. A young woman was staring pensively out of the window. She was sitting across the aisle from me and stared ahead, the neon lights radiating from the brightly coloured fast-food shops and signs casting a glow against her white powdered face and peroxide-blonde hair.

I jumped off the bus at a random location, stepping off the back of the bus just as it came to halt. Looking around, I had no idea where I was; I didn't even know which direction was home.

I started walking, wandering for miles in no particular direction, still without a clue how to get back. I started to get tired. Around the back of a row of shops, I spotted a dark stairwell leading to a block of flats. Underneath the concrete steps, there was a little space, tucked away from the world, out of sight and out of mind. I zipped up my coat and pulled up my hood, nestling down. I closed my eyes and tried to shut the world. I drifted off into a hazy half-sleep with a head full of nothing. This little corner of nowhere would become a regular retreat for me; I didn't know it then, but I would sleep under that stairwell many times.

'Who's that?' I whispered, waking with a start. 'Who's there?' Poking my head around the bottom of the stairs, I saw a little brown dog. He just stood there, passively staring at me and panting.

'Hello sweetheart,' I said to him softly, holding out my hand. 'Have you come to say hello to me?' But the dog just gave a little whimper, turned and trotted away. I got up and walked around to the café that I'd spotted on the row of shops in front of the tatty block of flats. Peering in through the shutters on the shop window, I could just make out a large clock on the wall at the back of the café. It was 3am. I'd been missing since about 7pm the evening before. I wondered if my mum and dad had even noticed that I had gone. I really felt like the invisible child.

Returning to my stairwell shelter, I shuffled about, trying to get comfortable, my bony backside hard against the cold concrete floor. Eventually, I started to nod off. I thought about the three Johns at the funfair. In my mind, I could see them dancing across the fast-moving rides with big, cheesy smiles on their faces, laughing and toying with all the people on the ride. Of course, by now they would be tucked up in nice beds, in their warm, cosy caravans, surrounded by happy faces with love in their hearts, and a full English breakfast with hot tea readied for them in the morning. If they were all called John, I wondered, what were all the girls in their family called?

The gentle sound of raindrops woke me again, so I walked back around to the café. It was still closed, but in any case, I had no money. The clock above the counter said 4.05am. The sign on the front door said the café opened at 6am. I thought about going home, but I really didn't think that would end well. Then, as I walked back towards the stairwell, I spotted a bus with 'Chingford' written on the front. I had an idea.

Retracing my steps, I eventually found my way back to familiar territory. Then, turning into my street, I hid in the bushes at the top of our road to avoid being spotted by the neighbours. I waited patiently, keeping a sharp eye out for my mum. The smell of stale beer and old cigarettes fused with the heady whiff of council disinfectant from the stair-well had seeped into all my dirty clothes. I stank, and my hair was already matted together with the combination of rain and sweat. Every part of me ached from sleeping on a cold concrete floor and I had a right headache, but I felt free.

Peeking through the privet bushes, my heart skipped a beat when I spotted the unmistakable figure of my mum in her blue coat as she stepped out of our neat three-bedroom semi and turned left down towards the bus stop. I wondered if she had even noticed that I wasn't at home.

'Right, Michelle,' I whispered to myself. 'Here's your big chance.'

Climbing over the fence at the side of my house, I let myself in through the kitchen door.

'Hello,' I shouted, just in case my dad or anybody else was home.

Running the bath, I dashed around the house like a girl possessed, looking for a few quid to keep me going. I couldn't take any chances, and I wasn't about to get caught. Scrubbing myself raw, I washed my greasy hair before riffling through my wardrobe and digging out my best Fruit of the Loom jumbo cords and my sparkly black top, stuffing my dirty clothes under the bed as I did so.

'Just time for a quick cheese sandwich,' I said, opening the fridge.

Pocketing a handful of coins from my piggy bank, I grabbed my coat and skipped out of the front door with that catchy Andy Williams song ringing in my head. I had survived my first night away from home, and had returned, recharged and was ready for anything. I felt like an outsider, free to do whatever I pleased, just as long as I could occasionally nip home to get a bath and some clean clothes. I could slip off into the wild blue yonder; well, I could follow the fair to Chingford, anyway!

Leapfrogging the underground barrier and disappearing into the crowds, I made my way on the tube to Walthamstow Central, and from there to Chingford, the next stop-off on the fairground's round of visits.

The journey across London was exciting. The blank faces on the tube made me laugh. To me, it looked like most of the other passengers were desperately trying to get somewhere that they really didn't want to go to! I'd never given it any thought before, but as I looked around, I began to see that the underground was such a strange place: so many faceless people, avoiding eye contact with all the other faceless people. We all sat or stood close together in a metal tube, in a dark tunnel, with one of the busiest places on earth a few feet above our heads, and none of us ever spoke to each other!

Jumping over the turnstiles at Chingford, I ran out of the station, terrified of getting caught by the guards. Once safely out, I made my way to the fair.

'Hello, you,' I said to John Junior, tapping him on the shoulder.

'Oh, hiya,' he said, surprised. 'You're the girl from Broomhill Park, aren't you?'

My heart sank – he couldn't remember my name. I wanted so desperately to be part of their transient life. Spending your life packing up and moving on to pastures new seemed like the perfect antidote to all those miserable faces I'd seen on the tube. I wanted that life – and I wanted to be accepted by all the Johns at the fair.

'Is it Penny?' he asked.

He was close; it was a start, and it was good enough for me.

'Penny was my friend,' I told. 'She was the girl I was with that night.'

'Of course,' he smiled. 'You're Michelle, aren't you? The girl in the white rah-rah skirt!'

Feeling like a genuine explorer out on a limb at the edge of the known universe, I stepped onto the Waltzers for a free ride courtesy of my new best friend, John.

Within no time at all, I'd been accepted into their world. I followed them around all over London, Essex, Surrey . . . Wherever they went, I'd find them. I even roped Penny into my escapades. Bunking off school and running away became of a part of my life. I had never before felt that sense of belonging, as if I was a part of something.

The dark places that haunted me wouldn't go away, though. The only release I ever found was being out on my own on the streets at night. I slept in hospital toilets, telephone boxes and derelict buildings. During the day, I would sneak home and pick up supplies before disappearing again. Time after time, the police would bring me home and give me and my mum a good talking-to in the front room, but as soon as I could, I would seize my opportunity and slope off to the back room to slip out of the window and away.

'Penny!' I half-shouted, half-whispered, as I lobbed tiny stones at her bedroom window. 'Penny, it's me!'

'Michelle!' she shrieked as she peered out into the darkness. 'What the bloody hell are you playing at?'

'Open the door.' I sniggered. 'I'm freezing out here.'

'What?'

'Open the flamin' door. I need somewhere to sleep.'

'You can't sleep here,' she mouthed in hushed tones, hanging out of her bedroom window. 'My mum and dad are in bed. It's two o'clock in the bloody morning.'

I could hear her dad snoring from out in the street. There was no way he was waking up. I could have banged on the front door like a bailiff, and he wouldn't have stirred. But I just couldn't face going back home. I didn't belong there. The fair had set up in Morden right at the end of the Northern Line, and I'd spent the day there having a laugh and hanging out with John Junior. But now it was cold, and I didn't fancy another night in the stairwell or in a phone box.

'Come on,' said Penny, silently opening her front door. 'Take off your shoes and don't make a sound.' Creeping up the stairs with my plimsolls in my hands, I sneaked into Penny's bedroom at the back of the house. All the way up, I could hear her dad's earth-shattering snores.

'Penny!' her mum suddenly shouted from inside her bedroom. 'Is that you?'

I was amazed she ever had any sleep with what sounded like a thundering locomotive train lying next to her.

'Yes,' she said. 'Just getting a glass of milk.'

'OK,' her mum said softly. 'Sleep tight, love.'

Holding my hand over my mouth, I battled desperately to stifle a fit of giggles bubbling up inside my belly. It was hilarious. Penny threw me a mock dirty look and shook her fist at me. Sleeping top to toe in her cosy bed, I felt safe and warm. As soon as her parents got up, I crawled under her bed and waited until they had left for work and Penny had set off for school, before slipping out of the back door and over her garden fence.

'You'll get me shot, you will,' she said as I caught up with her on the way to school.

'Jesus, your dad don't half snore' I laughed, linking her arm as we marched along the road. 'Are you coming to the fair today?'

'Got no money,' she replied, holding her empty pockets open.

'I've still got a few quid. We can jump on the tube and get on the rides for free. They're my mates now.'

'Really?' She beamed.

'Trust me.' I smiled.

We went into school and stayed until our names had been read out from the register. Afterwards, instead of going straight to a double period of maths, we ran across the playground, dived through a tiny gap in the school fence, and ran off. We spent the day at the fair and were back in time for tea.

The fairground gave me a welcome distraction from all the dark places in my life. Without a moment's thought for the dangers of sleeping rough and wandering the streets of London, I spent all my time following the fair around and hanging out with my new mates. Before long, I felt like one of their own, part of the family. New faces and new places opened up to me in a makeshift world of shifting environments and different days. While I was never in one place for very long, moving around gave me the security that I craved. I had a sense of belonging at last. The police brought me home time after time, and once even held me at the police station until my mum came to collect me. They'd found me asleep in a telephone box in the early hours of the morning on the other side of London. Wandering the streets of London at night as a troubled teenager was exciting and terrifying in equal measure. My mother was more concerned about how she looked in front of the police officers than she was for my own welfare.

As I looked around the busy London streets, I felt a strange kind of comfort in being lost, away from everything that I knew and everything that defined me as a person. With nowhere to go and nobody on my side, I felt as though I had nothing to lose, and consequently, I took risks that I would never dream of taking now. I feel certain that I must have been some sort of roaming wild animal in a previous life!

However, whether I was brought back or returned voluntarily, I always had my home base. No matter how much trouble I was in, home provided the opportunity to get clean and refuel before I took off again. I didn't know it at the time, but the restless, nomadic and occasionally adventurous life I had created for myself gave me valuable glimpses into the reality of lives lived by those with no homes to go back to, and this sowed seeds within me. Perhaps it was God, fate or some other force foreshadowing what was to come in my life, as if the hardships I was experiencing would prepare me for dedicating my life to helping others overcome their own difficulties.

One evening, early in my fairground following days, I was leaving the underground when, at the bottom of the escalator, I saw an old man propped up against the tube station wall. By his side, buried under a dirty old blanket, was his little white dog.

'Hello,' I said to him. 'What's your dog's name?'

'His name's Striker,' he said, with a worried look on his face. 'But don't tell anyone we're here, they'll kick me out, and it's nice and warm down here.'

'Really?' I asked, kneeling down to stroke Striker, a beautiful white mix of English Bull Terrier and Jack Russell. 'Why would they kick you out?' Striker's big brown eyes looked so sad; he whimpered and cosied up to me as I petted him. 'Why don't you just go home and sit in front of the fire?'

'This is my home.' The man smiled. 'And I haven't got a fire to sit by.'

'Where do you live, then?' I asked naively.

The man was much younger than he at first appeared. His face was worn, and his hair was long and straggly. I recognised the smell of fags, stale beer and sweat. It smelled like the stairwell at the flats where I'd slept many times. The man's legs were wrapped in the same blanket that Striker was hiding under, and he had a couple of plastic bags containing his things on the floor by his side.

'I live on the streets, love,' he said. 'I'm homeless.'

I was stunned, and if I'm honest, I'm not sure I believed him, or really understood what he was saying and what it all meant. Smiling at him, I wished him well and said goodbye to Striker, giving him a final stroke on the head.

CHAPTER 3

Feeding Time at the Zoo

The clock was ticking. I had a million and one things to do, and little or no time in which to do them. Just like on every other day in my crazy, mad house, I didn't make lists of things I needed to do – I had to make a list of the things I knew I wouldn't be able to fit in!

'Calm yourself, Bailey,' I told him as he burst into life at the very sound of me picking up his bowl. 'It's coming. Have I ever let you down? And you, Milly, d'you want yours?'

Bailey was such a lively, clever dog. Sometimes I think he could tell the time as well as read my mind! Hardly surprising, really; he had spent most of his life as a highly trained working dog, searching for bombs and sniffing out explosives for the Metropolitan Police EXPO Team. I had met him during my time working at the London Olympics. My job was in admin at the office, nothing like the high-pressure work Bailey did; his amazing skills and training helped to keep us all safe. I saw him every day, and we grew very close. At the end of the Games, he was about to be retired, but I'd become so close to him that I couldn't bear the thought of never seeing him again. I jumped at the chance to adopt him, and he became part of our family. I'm not sure Chez Clark would ever be considered as a terrorist target, but if Al Qaeda did set their sights on us, they would have my own little explosive Springer Spaniel superhero to contend with – and I know which side I'd rather be on!

Milly is my stunning three-year-old Maltese Terrier, a wonderful, joy-filled ball of fluff who exudes nothing but love and fun. She, too, is a rescue dog. My house is filled with waifs and strays; it's a good job my own kids understand the unconditional love that dogs and other animals can bring to a family. To be fair, they don't have much choice; they know I prefer the company of animals to humans, and to be honest, if they didn't like it, they'd just have to lump it!

Dashing around is what I do; it's who I am. I hate sitting and watching TV. Besides, I really haven't got the attention span. And even though I've written books myself, I still haven't finished reading the novel I've been trying to get through since 1999, preferring instead to spend my time looking after others with more pressing needs.

My cats are most definitely and uncompromisingly in charge. They sit patiently, biding their time, as cats do, always safe in the knowledge that I would never dream of not feeding them, nor would I ever leave the house without first making sure they had everything they needed – and a big cuddle. There's Lolly, Pickle (my naughty, mischievous little girl who is always getting into a right 'pickle') and, of course, Fweddie – yes, that's the correct spelling. He's such a lovely, affectionate fur baby; as soon as he arrived in my life, I picked him up and smothered him with love. Of course, he was a rescue cat, too.

A young girl from the local area who had been told that I was a soft touch for lost souls brought him to me. 'Hi Michelle, we have a lost little pussy here,' she said, handing me this tiny handful of black and white fur. 'His name is Freddie.' She smiled. 'Do you know anyone who could take him in?' Of course, she came to the right person – I will always make room for one more.

'Oh, my beautiful boy,' I said impulsively, as he fell into my arms. 'You're not Freddie, you're my 'ickle Fweddie, aren't you!' Like all the animals, he very quickly became an integral part of our family. And it seemed the right thing to do to keep calling him Fweddie!

Everybody in my neighbourhood, and even further afield, identifies me as the 'Crazy Cat Lady', and they all know that I just can't say no to an animal that needs some 'tender loving care' and a proper, loving home, despite the associated household chaos and the demands that accompany my reputation as a local emergency service for animals in need of help. First thing in the morning is like feeding time at the zoo in my house, but I think I have my priorities in order!

However, weighing heavily on my mind after caring for my flock is the torrent of emails and messages that inevitably come in overnight; I get flooded with them. Calls in the wee small hours too; they never seem to stop. But of course, my clients are night-time people. They are all alone with their dogs out on the unforgiving streets of London, twenty-four hours a day and seven days a week. This makes it difficult to say no when my phone goes off at four o'clock in the morning because some poor soul out there is having a crisis; whether they've lost their dog, been mugged, been beaten up or are struggling with their mental health.

The phone calls usually start with same opening gambit: 'I didn't wake you, did I, Michelle?'

A little voice in my head shouts and screams, 'No, I'm always up at this bloody time of the night! How about I call *you* at six o'clock in the morning, then?' But I never do. I tell them I was up anyway, and not to worry – as I pick the dried sleep from my eyes and reach for my bedside glass of water! Disrupted sleep, anxiety and the invisible, constant pressure to respond are essential aspects of the work my life has given me, and I have embraced them. They reflect experience that has been hard-won and provide continued evidence for the sad necessity of the charity I set up.

Dogs on the Streets is all about the needs of wandering spirits and their much-loved animals. It's not about me, and it's not about the countless, virtue-signalling do-gooders who stick their oars in for no other reason than to assuage their own consciences. For some out there, homelessness is a growth industry with a clearly defined career path! Some of the bitchiness and sheer bloody-mindedness of professional 'supporters' can leave me speechless, even after all these years of juggling the genuine needs of my clients against the self-righteous rulebooks of certain charities and government-funded initiatives. On top of all that, I get the daily joy of ploughing through the emails and social media posts from a multitude of keyboard warriors. They all seem to think nothing of dishing out advice they have gleaned from Facebook or Google, or sometimes from some bloke they got talking to down the pub. I get so many messages telling me what I should or shouldn't be doing, most of them from slacktivists and know-it-alls who think they're experts on homelessness without ever having left their sofas!

'Michelle, you are the most aggressive, nasty person I have ever come across,' read one such email. 'Watch your back because I'm coming for you.' Stifling my anger and laughing it off, I deleted it. This typically vitriolic message came from, of all people, an ex-homeless-service caseworker who thought they knew best. In truth, their mission is to stand between me and my clients and their dogs – the only ones who matter to me. My priority is to get these people and their animals supported, housed and cared for. Without a doubt, I deserve my reputation for not suffering fools gladly. I am feisty, bolshy, but I have to be in order to get things done. I will always stand up to anyone who takes it upon themselves to put hurdles in the way of my clients' welfare and that of their dogs.

Thankfully, negative nasties are more than balanced out by the very many good people out there who work their socks off to make life easier and do their very best to help. These kindred spirits are the backbone of Dogs on the Streets, sometimes even going the extra mile by paying for essentials out of their own pockets or sacrificing time away from family occasions like Christmas, Easter or summer holidays. I know how hard it can be doing battle with councils, agencies and bureaucrats, who sometimes view the homeless as a scourge on society and a drain on resources, when all too often they are actually vulnerable people who, for a multitude of different reasons, have been left by the wayside, abandoned or cast adrift, and left to fend for themselves. Every day in towns and cities across the country, countless thousands of people walk past individuals made invisible, simply part of the everyday street furniture – waste bins, lamp posts and notices – so familiar that we seldom consciously register them. When noticed at all, they are too often seen only as dirty and dishevelled outsiders who pose a threat to so-called 'normal' people and the fabric of urban society. Few of us, though, will go through life without experiencing cataclysmic events that are practically and emotionally destructive. Whatever the long-term impact of such terrible experiences, with the help of others and personal reserves of inner strength embedded in secure backgrounds, most of us will, somehow, survive. There are no guarantees, though, and even the strongest of us can find ourselves trembling at the edge of mental illness or becoming overwhelmed when things get too much. Life has a terrible habit of throwing up disastrous consequences to unexpected events, and when this happens, people can find themselves out on the streets. Very few choose to be homeless. Nobody wants to be down and out, cold and hungry, unloved and uncared for. This is not a lifestyle choice; it's a last resort.

Day after day and night after night, I trawl through the city streets, checking on my clients, making sure they have enough to eat, checking they've got blankets and proper clothing, and ensuring their dogs are not having to go without food or proper care. My own two kids hardly ever see me; I am always on the go or racing off somewhere. There are days when it seems that every time I sit down, I am called out again. Even if I'm not on the move, I can't sit still; I have to keep busy. If there isn't some awful tragedy or an emergency with one of my clients that takes me away from home, I still have to be doing something. I have always felt compelled to fill every empty space, and the demands of juggling family life with my outside work have made this an essential part of getting by. I never waste a minute of any day; if I do have a spare moment, I fill it by running the vacuum cleaner over the carpet or tackling the endless piles of washing and ironing that never seem to get any smaller!

Sitting at my keyboard, as you can see, often gets me really wound up. I have to read through every message that comes in, because buried in the mounds of codswallop, there are some very important things that need to be dealt with. If I am not careful, vital despatches and communications from some of the fantastic organisations Dogs on the Streets works alongside can easily be lost in a sea of junk. We are in constant touch with devoted workers from places like St Mungo's and Connections, to name but two, as well as the kind-hearted souls who email me to offer up their time for nothing. We would be nowhere without the genuine altruism of the army of volunteers who step up to the plate to help. We have drivers, vets, dog groomers, mechanics, cab drivers; people from all walks of life who want to chip in and do their bit.

One day, as I scrolled through my inbox, a new message from Facebook came in.

'Hi Michelle. You don't know me, but I was told you might be able to help. There is a homeless man who sleeps outside the station opposite my apartment. He got sick last night, and the paramedics took him to hospital. But they refused to take his dog in the ambulance, so I took it in. We have him here. Can you help?'

'Yes, of course,' I typed furiously. 'Send me your address and I will call and collect him. I have to go into London but can be there at teatime. Is that OK?'

'Yes. Thank you so much.'

'One more thing.' My thumbs of fury tapped at my keyboard faster than a teenager on Snapchat. 'What's his name?'

'Kaizer,' she replied. 'And his owner is called Arthur.' Grabbing my coat and my bag, I dashed out of the door, jumped into my trusty little Fiesta and headed off towards the city.

CHAPTER 4

Crossroads at Crouch End

Driving through the streets of London, I would habitually stare into the throngs that mill around the city and wonder where all these people had come from and where they were going. The beeping of car horns, the rumble of buses and the wail of police sirens reverberated and bounced off the buildings. Layers of city grime clung to everything and everyone, permeating through clothing to the skin. The air was heavy with diesel fumes and the stench of fast-food shops.

'Get out of my way, you silly moo,' I shouted, beeping my horn, as a young girl stepped out right in front of me. The traffic was crazy, even for London. The pavements were so crowded, and the roads were packed, bumper to bumper. The carefree and the reckless were marching out into the middle of the road as if they were indestructible. It was coming up to rush hour, and the usual irritated masses were pouring in and out of underground stations like synchronised zombies. Drivers with blank faces were battling through impossible traffic just to get to jobs they didn't like for a wage that was never enough. Commuters, doing the same things in the same places at the same time every day. Half-asleep workers queueing at bus stops, standing in line every morning with the same individuals, never even saying 'Good morning' to each other, let alone knowing each other's names. Countless numbers were hurrying and scurrying in all directions like static electricity, while others shuffled slowly through the day on autopilot. And, like the fool that I am, I was here as well, battling through the incessant rat race at this ridiculous time of the day, on my way to rescue a stranded dog from a dire state of affairs.

Setting off on fraught missions like this is nothing out of the ordinary for me. It seems like every day offers a distinctive drama and a new journey into the unknown. The details I had been given were very scant, and I didn't even know the full name of Kaizer's owner – whether he was one of my existing clients or what exactly his situation was. All I knew was that this man was obviously very sick, and that he would almost certainly be fretting about his dog. That's why we're here – we look after the defenceless animals that loyally stay with their owners through thick and thin. It's the least we can do.

'OK, bear with me, I'll get someone there as soon as I can.' I spoke into my handsfree car kit. Another call had come in: another situation where a homeless person had found everything too much to cope with. 'I'm on my way to Westminster, but one of our volunteers will be with you very shortly.'

'OK, Michelle, thanks,' the caller said. 'It's a young girl who seems to have overdosed. She has a terrier-type dog who is standing over her, refusing to budge.'

A police officer had very kindly agreed to wait with a young woman who had passed out on a street in North Finchley. I called one of our angelic volunteers to go over and rescue the poor little dog, while I drove on into town. Jobs were piling up and the day was getting busy. Calls kept coming in, and texts, messages and emails were pulling me in different directions. I had to focus.

Then, as the traffic came to a halt at the roundabout at the bottom of Park Road, near the Clock Tower in Crouch End, I spotted something that made me shed a little nostalgic tear. A young man was propped up against the wall outside Waitrose. He was covered in blankets and had the cutest little Staffie huddled into his side. I had no idea who he was, I'd never seen him before, but my heart melted at the very sight of him. For me, this was a special place: where it all had begun.

The journey that led me to work with homeless people and ultimately saw me making the decision to dedicate my life to supporting the dispossessed had started with a fateful meeting at that very spot. This was the place where I had stopped to talk to Kenneth and his little Staffie, Prince. It was years ago, but it seemed like only yesterday. Though I'd seen them before, something had made me stop and talk to Kenneth and Prince that day. They were sitting on the pavement in their regular spot in the doorway of the same supermarket where another young man was now sitting. That day changed my life for ever. It was that experience which compelled me to dedicate my life to helping desperate people on the streets in all kinds of weather; people who are starving, cold and sick, and all alone in the world, except for their cherished dogs.

Looking back, I have learned so much since then, not just about homelessness, but about human nature; not only how cruel people can be to each other, but also how kind, with strangers going out of their way and giving so much of themselves to help. It was freezing cold and only a matter of days before Christmas 2013. Kenneth told me he was homeless. At the time, I still didn't really understand what that truly meant, or how somebody could possibly end up living out their whole life on the streets. It all seemed so completely alien to me, so out of the ordinary and unnecessary. In my naivety, I imagined our social care system, the NHS and local councils would provide food, shelter and basic necessities rather than allow somebody to fend for themselves and sleep out on the pavements. Surely all the endless taxes we pay every year should be able to fund a way to cater for the desperate and the needy in society? I remembered somebody telling me that the measure of a society is how we treat the vulnerable, and increasingly, it looked to me like we were simply not measuring up.

I passed Kenneth and Prince every day as I rushed around picking up supplies and dropping off goods for the online pet accessory business I was then running. Back then, I thought my day-to-day life was busy, but I had no idea; compared to the way things are now, those days were a cinch. I can still see Prince's beautiful little face when I stooped down to pet him and give him the doggie treats I'd bought for him. They were both thrilled, but most of all, I think, Kenneth was happy that somebody had noticed him and treated him like a human being. Thinking back to my days as a teenage runaway, following John and the fair all over the place, I remembered what it was like to be out in the cold and sleeping on a concrete floor. I was fortunate, though: I had no understanding of what the experience of sleeping rough would be like if you didn't have the option of going home. My troubles seemed to pale into insignificance in comparison.

Shoppers walked straight past me and Kenneth as we chatted that day. They all had their heads bowed down, almost as if they didn't want to acknowledge the human misery that was happening right in front of their eyes. Feeling guilty that I hadn't bought anything for Kenneth,

I was torn apart inside as he told me how he had ended up living on the streets.

Kenneth and Prince made me realise the scale of the problem, not just in London but in the country as a whole. At the time, I was juggling being a busy mum and working for myself. I'd race through my days at breakneck speed in order to get back home in time for my kids, more often than not stopping off at a supermarket somewhere to pick up something for tea. The list of things to do got longer and longer: filling up the car, doing my accounts, cooking dinner, doing the washing, getting through the housework and paying all the bills. I rushed from one thing to another, trying to pack everything in without forgetting anything. But the more I raced around the city, thinking about my experience with Kenneth and Prince, the more I started to notice all the other rough sleepers out on the streets. Like hidden ghosts, they melted into the background; ever-present but rarely noticed, let alone properly looked at or considered; a bit like the many statues dotted around the capital, they just became part of the taken-for-granted, practically invisible urban landscape. Within a matter of days, I realised that homelessness was an epidemic of enormous proportions and something drastic needed to be done.

As I had walked away from Kenneth and Prince on the first day we met, I remember he called after me. 'Michelle, Michelle,' he shouted up the street as I made my way back to my car. 'This was our lucky day, wasn't it? We were just where we needed to be today!'

I struggled to see how Kenneth was in any way lucky. I knew even then that day wasn't about luck. I felt as if something or someone had put me there, as if it was meant to be. I knew with certainty that the resolve I felt walking away from those two poor souls was very deep inside me, and in the days and weeks after, it just kept getting stronger and stronger. No matter how hard I tried to distract myself, I couldn't take my mind away from the horrific experiences of want and deprivation endured by the homeless, who were to be found all around me. The smell of the concrete stairway I'd slept under as a teenage runaway came back to haunt me. That stomach-churning stench of ground-in sweat, stale cigarettes, urine and disinfectant became all-pervasive, and I couldn't shake off the vivid images that were endlessly flashing through my mind. The more I thought about that particularly unpleasant smell, the more it seemed to follow me around. I could smell it everywhere.

My life had always reflected a search for what I now see as a sense of purpose. As a teenager, I had so many different little jobs, from working in shops to getting up at the crack of dawn down at the market, to washing cars, mowing lawns and walking dogs. I had more jobs than you could shake a stick at! That didn't change as I got older; in fact, I got busier. Being a mother of two, and entrepreneurially self-employed alongside running a home, rarely left me with time to think and to be honest, this is probably what

what drove me. Fear of thinking too much. I was so afraid of my own thoughts and my own traumas, I threw myself into looking after others as a way of self-healing. If I was unhappy with my work, I would change it, or move on to another challenge, constantly chopping and changing. If what I was doing was bringing me no satisfaction, I did something about it. I never hesitated to try a new approach or to start up yet another sideline, probably in the hope that I'd find something that would feel more like 'me'. Before my pet accessory business, I had worked on the London Olympics; before that, I'd had sunbed shops, minicabs, a baby shoes business, a delivery firm; all manner of ways to keep busy and keep on moving. Throughout my life, I have faced many difficulties. In fact, when I think about it, there is very little I *haven't* been through! Facing my battles has made me a stronger person, and it has left me tougher and ready to confront whatever comes my way.

On that day it was Kaizer and his owner who were the priority. Leaving Crouch End and the memory of Kenneth and Prince, I said a little prayer for both of them and pressed on to the West End.

CHAPTER 5

Poppy's Legacy

That initial meeting with Kenneth and Prince opened my mind to the relationships that so many of those living on the streets forge with the animals who become their constant companions. I began to see homeless people in a whole new light, and this ultimately led to my fateful meeting with Tom the gentle giant, owner of Poppy the Street Dog, the little Staffie who changed my life completely. Without her, Dogs on the Streets would never have happened, so many people would be so much worse off, and I just don't know what direction my life would have taken. Poppy and I were destined to meet. Sometimes I think it doesn't matter what road you choose; it always leads you to the place where you were meant to be. In my case, the road led me to Poppy and a future dedicated to helping homeless people and their dogs.

Tom was distraught when I met him that fateful day at the St Martin-in-the-Fields church in Trafalgar Square. He explained that, through no fault of his own, he had become separated from the only friend he had in the world – his beloved dog, Poppy. She had been swallowed up into the system and was completely lost to him. Tom had not even the faintest idea of how to find out what had become of her, let alone how to try and get her back. Poppy was out there on her own, away from the one person who returned the unconditional love she gave.

Tom's story of how he and Poppy had become separated was, I later came to recognise, an all-too-common tale. Tom had collapsed close to Victoria station. Poppy was found sitting on top of him, licking his face and crying. Loyal and protective, she refused to leave his side. In the end, the police were brought in to take her away so that the ambulance service could work on Tom and eventually ferry him off to hospital. When Tom was ultimately released, no one could tell him what had happened to Poppy – she had been taken away with the best intentions, but both she, and Tom as her owner, had then been forgotten about. Hearing his story and seeing how utterly bereaved he was by the loss of his companion, no one could have remained unmoved. My heart bled for him, and I was desperate to help. Despite my best efforts calling around everywhere I could think of, though, I could find neither sight nor sound of Tom's precious dog. Looking for a lone Staffordshire Bull Terrier in a vast metropolis can be daunting, and without any real starting point, it was like looking for a needle in a haystack. At the time, poor Tom was completely overwhelmed, with no idea where his dog had been taken or by whom. The police were no help, and neither were social services. They had their own heavy caseloads to look after and were unable to dedicate time or energy to finding a missing dog. Poppy was nowhere to be seen, and I began to despair that I could do nothing to reunite her with her owner.

Then, a few weeks later and completely out of the blue, I got a breakthrough. A support worker from the charity Lost Connections approached me while I was at the annual service of commemoration for those who had died out on the streets in the past year, held at St Martin's in the Field. People from all walks of life – charity workers, outreach workers, support staff, police officers, members of the public and the homeless people themselves – get together and remember the poor unfortunate souls who have died on the streets of London. It is always a very moving and worthwhile event, which offers a moment of quiet reflection and one that I try hard to attend every year.

'Hi Michelle,' said Sharon, a homelessness support worker I'd known for some time. 'I've been looking all over for you.'

I smiled. 'What's up?'

'You've been looking for that little Staffie who was sitting on the chest of that tiny, thin man who collapsed at Victoria a few months back, haven't you?'

'Yes, I have,' I answered, a bit surprised. 'His name is Tom, and he came looking for me after somebody told him I'd be able to help him find his dog. But I can't seem to get a lead on her. It's as if she's vanished into thin air. Why do you ask – have you heard something?'

'Tom discharged himself before the police got to the hospital. He's been out looking for the dog ever since. We found him some temporary accommodation as he has been really unwell. But he just keeps crying about his dog and saying he's scared he'll never see his best friend ever again.'

'I know, I've got to know him,' I told her. 'He is ever such a nice fella, so softly spoken and caring.'

'Well, it's like this – I saw a Facebook post about it the other day,' she said, leaning in conspiratorially. 'I'd heard on the grapevine that you were looking for that Staffie. Then I was tagged in a post that might be useful to you. A group of people connected to a rescue centre who have started taking in strays and abandoned dogs from the police in the Victoria area were chatting about it. The posts were disgusting. They were talking about a dog that had been brought to them; a dog called Poppy that the police had taken from a down-and-out who had caused a commotion outside Victoria station. They said he had been arrested and that the police had taken the dog and kept it at their kennel. Nobody had come forward to claim her, so the dog was eventually brought to their charity ahead of being rehomed as a rescue dog.' Sharon told me the posts had been vitriolic, calling Poppy's owner 'a useless crackhead and spice addict' and saying that he 'should be shot'.

To say that I was appalled would be a gross understatement. In addition to these people publishing a completely inaccurate, garbled story of Poppy's history, damning the character of a man they had never met and presenting a narrative of what had happened to him that bore no resemblance to the truth, the effort I had put into tracing Poppy had failed. All that time she'd been there, waiting to be 'rescued'.

I stared open-mouthed at Sharon, momentarily shocked into horrified silence. 'But I have called literally every police station in London looking for that dog!' I raged, once I could speak again. 'And I definitely called the police at Victoria Embankment and Belgravia. Nobody there told me anything.'

'You know how it can be,' she said. 'For most coppers, there are other more pressing matters to be dealt with – and, deep down, there isn't the time or the resources to look after cases like this. It's tough out there; people get robbed, attacked in the street, raped and murdered. Nobody really cares about a missing dog, and one belonging to a homeless man at that.'

'No, but honestly,' I protested. 'Where do these people get off? Tom is a human being with feelings. He loves that dog and would do anything for her. She is all he has.'

As soon as I left the memorial service, I called the police at Victoria and demanded to know where Poppy had been taken. They gave me the name of the rescue place and a contact number. Walking along the streets of the West End on my way back to my car, I held my phone to my ear and called the rescue centre as I marched through the crowds. By the time I got back to where my car was parked, I was still on hold. Then, after getting in and setting off, the phone connected to my Bluetooth system. I got all the way to the North Circular Road before a voice finally came on the line.

'Hi, my name is Michelle Clark,' I said in my best professional-sounding voice. 'I'm enquiring about a dark brindle Staffie called Poppy that you took in from the police after an incident at Victoria a few months back.'

'Oh yeah,' the gruff voice on the line sneered.

I could immediately tell that this wasn't going to be straightforward.

'Yes, I have been working with Poppy's owner,' I continued in the politest tone that I could muster. 'We have been searching all over London for her. He is desperate to—'

'You ain't getting this dog, love,' he interrupted, talking over me and instantly cutting me dead. 'She's ours now, and we have found a perfectly good home for her where she will be safe, away from the streets and the druggie who was supposed to be looking after her.'

'But Poppy is his dog, and she is all he has got,' I pleaded.

'Listen, he is not having the dog, and neither are you,' he snarled. 'And that's the end of it.'

With the hairs on the back of my neck bristling with rage and my shoulders thrown back in a war-like stance, I let him have it. Typically for me, I wasn't going to stand for anyone talking about my clients like that and assuming ownership of Tom's dog, so I gave him both barrels of my wrath, tore a right strip off him and told him in no uncertain terms that I would be back.

Straight away, I called the Homeless Commissioner for Westminster, who I'd got to know really well by that time, having been in dozens of meetings with him, alongside other agencies including St Mungo's and Lost Connections. As a hands-on, boots-on-the-ground volunteer with lots of experience, one of my main objectives was always getting hostels to provide support for clients while I supported their dogs. Slowly, agencies were beginning to realise that they would never get some people off the streets unless they allowed their dogs into the shelters, the temporary accommodation and Westminster's contracted hostels. It was increasingly recognised that I would be there every step of the way, intervening and supporting the animals as well as their owners, and that I would continue with that support for as long as it was needed.

Through all the endless meetings and case conferences with the agencies, charities and local government, I came to learn a great deal about how the system works and, more importantly, where it falls down. One of the things I picked up was that if an agency provided support for a homeless person, they then had a duty of care, not only to them, but also to their possessions. And dogs came under the category of possessions. So that was a little loophole I could use to shift the balance of the argument in Tom's favour. He was now a client in a contracted hostel that happened to be in Westminster, thus Westminster City Council had a duty of care to his belongings. In Tom's case, these included his dog, Poppy.

For a multitude of reasons, many who become homeless inevitably descend on Central London. Those who arrive with some belief that this is a positive move quickly realise that the streets are not paved with gold, and that life in the capital for rough-sleepers can be very unforgiving. This was especially so for those who brought their dogs with them. As I pressed harder and harder, one or two hostels began opening up and allowed the homeless and their dogs into their shelters; ultimately, common sense dictated that they had to. However, providing access opened up a range of issues for them that they had not initially anticipated. Some of the caseworkers were naive in relation to their responsibilities under the Animal Welfare Act 2006. Obviously, this was not their fault – it was simply a matter of education. This is when I started offering tuition about how to approach people with dogs and the modifications in provision needed to accommodate the particular needs of pet-owner clients. Crucially, I was able to explain the Animal Welfare Act and what was expected of them while a dog was under their roof. It was essential that if, for any reason, a dog became embroiled in any kind of traumatic situation involving a homeless owner with a complex personality, mental health issues and addiction, they were equipped to deal with it. If they felt the dog was not being looked after, they would have a duty to speak up for that animal. Otherwise, they could be held accountable.

There is always the fear that if you don't comply with what a person you are supporting wants, they can easily become defensive and hostile; but, usually, at the end of the day, you both want the same thing. And if a situation arises where the dog is taken out of the equation or not considered in order to attempt to appease, calm or placate the owner, I will then step in and advocate for the dog. Bizarrely, as a result of this, I am often resented and sometimes disliked by caseworkers because of how vigorously and single-mindedly I defend and support the dogs.

My credibility was high within Westminster as they could see that I was proactively delivering a vital service to the homeless community. They got behind me when I discovered Poppy's fate, and went back to the police to demand their intervention. They needed to request the rescue centre return Poppy to them, and then they, in turn, would sign her over to me. They did just that, and I was able to take Poppy home with me.

After all the distress and upset she had been through, it was hardly surprising that she wasn't in a good state. She was visibly stressed, and in need of a good, warm, soapy bath and some intensive grooming. Very quickly, Poppy became part of the family. She was no trouble and always seemed so calm and passive; she was friendly with children and good-natured. As it turned out, the hostel that had accepted Tom could not accommodate Poppy, so she stayed with me. Several times a week, I would take her into Central London to meet up with Tom at a park or some other outdoor space. Their unbreakable bond of unconditional love was clearly evident as both their eyes lit up and each sprang into life as soon as they caught sight of each other.

As the weeks passed, I could see that Tom was getting itchy feet. It's one thing finding somewhere for a homeless man like to Tom live, but it can be quite a challenge getting him to stay there. For those who have spent time on the streets, the simple provision of shelter, although welcome and clearly essential, does not necessarily address the multitude of issues that made them homeless in the first place. Moreover, despite the hardships and real physical misery associated with living rough, men and women barely surviving on the streets can come to accept their situation as freeing them from 'burdens' associated with mainstream society, and might come to believe that alternatives are not for them. Eventually, and almost inevitably, Tom announced that he was leaving his hostel room and going back on the streets. Clearly this wasn't a good idea for Poppy, so reluctantly, he handed her over to my full-time foster care. Poppy and I had to watch him walk away. I was crying my eyes out, as was Poppy, as he turned his back on us, disappearing into the crowds.

That day left me with an even greater resolve and, looking deep into Poppy's eyes, I made a solemn pledge to spend the rest of my days helping the homeless and doing my best to alleviate the suffering of lost souls and their innocent animals. She made me realise that the connection homeless people had with their dogs was a very special one. They gave up so much in order to be with their pets, and the love and care they showed each other was a special kind of bond forged in love and togetherness.

About eighteen months later, and having had the very best care and love, Poppy passed away peacefully from cancer. Her legacy lives on in the form of Dogs on the Streets, or DOTS, as we call it, and we now operate weekly in London, as well as running regular services in other cities across the country. Our greatest hope is to continue our expansion, bringing our experience and support to as many areas as possible.

I managed to set up DOTS as a registered charity, and an army of volunteers very quickly got on board. We have a fully equipped mobile veterinary surgery vehicle, allowing ease of access to dogs in need. DOTS provides all the essential items and services animals are likely to need: health care, food, new harnesses and leads, plus training and grooming, are provided free each and every week. None of this would have happened were it not for the bright shining star that was Poppy the Street Dog.

CHAPTER 6

Connecting the DOTS

Tackling the 'homeless problem' has long been on the agendas of city councils throughout the country, although initiatives to address the issue, while often worthy, have not always been as successful as hoped for. As mentioned before, London has historically attracted people from all over the country, Europe and the world, who flock here for many different reasons. However, the city has not always been kind to those hoping for a new future, as so many lost souls have found to their cost. For these, walking the streets and sleeping rough can quickly become a way of life. Also, and unsurprisingly, London continues to be a magnet for those made homeless in other parts of the country. From experience, I know that when somebody's life has fallen apart and they have no one to turn to and nowhere to go, the least they can hope for is to be less alone. This, I think, is one of the main reasons why the homeless make their way to London, where there are many more like them; safety in numbers, so to speak. Whatever the individual narratives that accompany each rough-sleeper, though, their presence on the streets of Central London is only too visible for those who have eyes to see.

For decades, Westminster City Council has come under a lot of pressure from big department stores, exclusive haute-couture boutiques and tourist chiefs who want to keep the streets clean, drug-free and crime-free. These groups have traditionally sought only one solution to the 'problem'. Their main aim has been to have homeless people moved on in order to clear the way for 'normal' people with money to spend. However, Westminster City Council has come to accept that in a metropolis like London, no matter how desirable that aim might seem, it could never be achieved. As a consequence, they have adopted a different, more open-minded approach to the problem of homelessness.

In particular, the local powers-that-be have become a bit more understanding and willing to listen to the grass-roots charities like DOTS supporting the London homeless community. The Homeless Commissionaires lets me have free parking so I can get right into the heart of London, pull up anywhere in the West End and thus have access to the heavily populated areas where it is ordinarily impossible to park. Typically wedging my car into the tiniest of gaps, I proceed to empty it of the ludicrous number of bags I always carry round. In no time at all, I went from the 'crazy cat lady' to the 'crazy bag lady', and am now a familiar fixture on the streets of London. I must look a right sight as I make my way through the narrow streets of Soho, weighed down with far too many shopping bags, as well as my massive backpack, all loaded with supplies: drinks, sandwiches and blankets, as well as the all-important doggie treats and socks, the number one item requested by homeless people. These days, I never leave the house without half a dozen extra pairs of socks!

'All right, Michelle,' said a familiar voice from one of the ever-present stalls near Covent Garden. 'You out saving souls again, my love?'

'Ha, no rest for the wicked,' I said to her as I scurried past.

'Mind how you go, darlin',' she said, smiling as she continued serving a customer.

Stopping at a couple of tents pitched up nearby, I poked my nose inside. 'Hiya, Bob,' I said. 'How are you today?'

'Oh, fine thanks, Michelle,' he smiled.

'Read anything good recently?' I asked.

'Nothing quite as good as your book, Michelle.' He laughed.

'Cheeky.' I smiled as I handed him a fresh blanket and a packet of sandwiches, as well as some treats for his dog.

'Are you bringing Star to the mobile grooming unit later this week?' I asked.

'For sure, Michelle, he could do with a makeover and a good fluffing, thanks.' Bob smiled.

Star, his beautiful little crossbreed terrier, was nestled tightly into Bob's side as he folded the corner of the page and put down his book in order to chat to me. Bob was an avid bookworm, something unusual amongst the clients I work with. He can always be found on the streets of the West End, sitting on the pavement next to Star, with his head in a book. Whether it's a novel, a biography or true-life crime, he'll devour it – anything he can get his hands on.

Bob's story is heartbreaking, though sadly not uncommon. So many people are dangerously close to poverty and destitution, and a run of bad luck can push some beyond the point of no return. He had lost his job and started to struggle to make ends meet. Then he got behind with the rent and couldn't pay his bills, and the debts started piling up. The economic pressures on the family unit created tensions in Bob's relationship with his wife. Worry over money caused arguments, which increasingly turned into furious rows. Inevitably by this time struggling with his mental health, their relationship fractured, and they split up. Bob found himself alone. Within a very short space of time, circumstances had overwhelmed him, and he went from having a job, a wife, a nice home and a future, to nothing at all. With no other option, he started wandering the streets, sleeping rough and begging for mere pennies in order to survive. The bright lights of London drew him in, and he has been a wandering soul in the big, cold city for many years.

Several years ago, when I first met Bob, he told me that he took great comfort in reading. He had become such a regular feature of the areas he inhabited that, in addition to the odd sandwich, pound coin or cup of tea, some people would stop and hand him books that they'd set aside for him. He told me his favourite writer was Martina Cole, and to look out for copies of her books for him while I was on my travels. Being the ignoramus that I am, I'd never heard of her, even though she's one of Britain's top crime writers! That night, all those years back, I googled her name and found out that she was a local girl from Essex who had written dozens of best-selling books about London's gangster underworld. She is a patron not only of the single-parent charity Gingerbread, but also of Women's Aid. It was obvious to me that she was a caring woman with a big, big heart, so I decided to try to contact her and let her know about her biggest fan, Bob.

Within days of me sending her a note on Twitter, she had messaged back, and seemed genuinely interested and very compassionate. Days later, a box of her books arrived, all signed, for Bob and Star. He was so thrilled when I handed them to him, together with a personal letter from Martina Cole herself. It made both our days!

'Mind how you go, Bob.' I smiled as I patted Star. 'You've got my number if you need anything.'

'Thanks for the sandwiches, Michelle,' he said.

As I snaked my way through the packed tourist areas, the sun was beating down and the air was thick. Happy, smiling faces passed me on the walk to Leicester Square. The sound of 'Shotgun' by George Ezra filled the concourse as I walked over to greet a new face.

'Hello.' I smiled, kneeling down in front of the young man and his companion. 'I haven't seen you here before. My name is Michelle, and I run a service called Dogs on the Streets.'

'Oh, OK, hello Michelle,' he said. 'I'm Michael. Dogs? Is that what you call us?'

He had the most beautiful, mellifluous Irish accent, but a sadness in his eyes. While it was clear to me that Michael was high on some sort of substance, I would never judge a person for this. Drug and alcohol abuse are rife amongst the homeless, and most, if not all, have some sort of mental health issue too. Spice is the scourge of the streets. It is so cheap and readily available that it's hard for people sleeping rough not to dive headfirst into that twilight world of oblivion, where the unbearable becomes bearable, where pain and discomfort detach, and the illusion is created that they are successfully dealing with the harsh situation in which they have found themselves. Spice is a powerful influence.

'Nooooo, not at all.' I laughed. 'We look after the interests and needs of homeless people who also have dogs. I know how important a dog is. What's this fella's name?'

'His name's Judge,' Michael said, mustering a smile. 'We've been together since the start. He really is my best friend. Problem is, nowhere will take me in for the night because of him.'

Judge was sitting quietly, but panting in the heat. I bent down to stroke him, and began to pour him a bowl of water from the bottles I carry. He was a beautiful old Staffie, pure white and with a loving sense about him. 'Keep that bowl, Michael, it's sure to come in handy on a hot, sunny day like this,' I said as I handed him a few bottles of water and some sandwiches. 'We have a mobile vet station parked up on The Strand, outside Charing Cross police station. It's there every Sunday afternoon. You can't miss us; we stand out like a sore thumb! Bring Judge along any time, if he needs any treatment or jabs.'

'Thanks. I'll definitely bear it in mind, Michelle,' he said. 'You should speak to my dad, too.'

'Your dad?' I asked. 'Why's that?'

'He's also on the streets. That's him with his dog, sitting over there.'

Michael pointed towards the entrance to Leicester Square tube station. From a distance, I could see the family resemblance. Michael certainly was a chip off the old block; he looked just like his father.

'His name is Michael, too.' He smiled. 'But everyone calls him Mick and me Michael. His dog is called Spud. But be careful; he can be a bit snappy.'

At that time of day, with the sun beating down and the tourists in full-on spend mode, Leicester Square and its surrounding streets can give you a clear view of the scale of the homeless problem – they are everywhere, hiding in plain sight. Day-trippers and sightseers, milling about in all directions, were eating ice creams and sitting in the early summer sun. The sound of music from the shops and the various attractions clashed with that of the buskers and street entertainers, and the air was thick with the pungent smells of fast food and fumes. Everywhere, tourists and Londoners with bright faces and money to spend, looking for fun, could be seen laughing and enjoying all that this vibrant capital has to offer. Homeless people inevitably congregate in hectic locales such as this. Leicester Square, teeming with life, crowds pouring in and out, is one of the city's top spots for street begging.

Battling my way through the crowds towards the station, I approached Mick. I could see instantly that he was a substance abuser, like his son. Those familiar glazed eyes and a telling, faraway look, plunged into a void where the pain of the past cannot reach them.

'Hi there.' I smiled as I stooped down to shake his hand. 'How are you both doing today?'

Mick's own lovely little white Staffie looked quiet and timid, quite the opposite of how young Michael had described him.

'I'm not doing any harm.' Mick reacted with anger. 'Leave me alone.'

'It's OK,' I said, holding out my palms. 'I'm a friend. I'm here to help you and your beautiful dog.'

'What d'you want with me?' he said, slurring his words.

'I've got food and blankets, as well as supplies for your dog,' I replied. 'I'm on your side.'

Holding out some dog treats, I patted his dog and made a fuss of him. 'He's lovely,' I said. 'What's his name?'

'Spud.' Mick smiled.

Clearly a damaged individual, Mick quickly softened when he saw how Spud and I had instantly become friends.

'You've got a good way with animals, my love,' he said. Like his son, he had a smooth Irish accent. 'He's not the friendliest of beasts, normally. But he really seems to like you.'

'Oh, I don't mind,' I said. 'I love animals. Especially dogs.' I told Mick all about Dogs on the Streets, the grooming van and the mobile vet station. He quickly warmed to me, telling me that Spud needed some help. He thought the dog might even have fleas embedded under his skin.

'But the worst thing is his temper.' Mick sighed. 'He's fine with people, but when another dog appears on the scene, he completely loses the plot. He gets really angry, so I have to sit away from my own son, Michael, because Spud is always attacking poor little Judge. But he's my best friend, he looks after me, so I need to look after him, too. Can you help him, Michelle?' he said, looking longingly into my eyes, his words fracturing with unbridled emotion.

'Of course we can, Mick,' I said, smiling, handing him a packet of sandwiches and a drink. 'We have access to many kennels in an emergency. In fact, I live in and around dogs of all sorts and breeds all of the time. Some of them are really quite damaged and can lash out at times. But like any of us, dogs can sometimes snap when they are frightened. It's understandable. At Dogs on the Streets, we have a lady who comes in to work with the dogs using animal psychology. She uses all sorts of weird and wonderful methods to help them, and even reads to them to help calm them down. It's amazing; maybe Spud could come along sometime? We can help you too, Mick.'

The look in his eyes as I engaged with him was so telling. He was filling with emotion, and no doubt battling to contain the hurt inside him. I could see he was a very damaged man. I told him that I'd been speaking to Michael and Judge. 'What happened to you, Mick?' I asked. 'How come you both ended up on the streets?'

Confused, but touched that somebody had reached out and taken an interest in him and his son, Mick started explaining how their lives had fallen apart after the tragic death of Mary, his wife and Michael's mother. She'd died suddenly, and the shock had sent the two into a spiral of despair. Stricken with grief, Mick couldn't get himself going and was increasingly failing to turn up for work. Within a very short space of time, his life fell to rack and ruin. Unable to pay his bills, with debts piling up, no food in the cupboard, and no heating or lighting, he eventually lost the family home. Without a roof over his head and with nowhere to go, he and his son decided to walk away from it all – and just kept on walking, in no particular direction and without a destination; travelling around Ireland, searching for something that they could never find.

Like many in similarly desperate situations, and thinking the streets of London would offer opportunities not available in Ireland, Michael decided to seek out his brother-in-law. Sean had left Ireland many years before and gone to the capital to find work on building sites. Begging on the streets, the two Michaels had raised enough money to pay for the ferry across the Irish Sea. They then made their way south in search of a new start and a better life, hoping to find jobs, a home and new identities. But sadly, it didn't work out for them. Sean's exile had not brought him security, and they ended up joining him on the streets.

'So, there are three members of your family living on the streets?' I asked.

'Yes, that's right,' he said. 'Me, Michael and Sean. And we all have dogs.'

Their story was typical in many ways but no less tragic. I'd seen it a thousand times before, but despite this, I never could detach myself fully from the tragedy of such a situation. I thought of my own experiences of feeling like an outsider: a square peg in a round hole, not fitting in anywhere. My teenage years, spent drifting around London and the south-east, haunted and inspired me in equal measure.

Mick and Michael had made a real impression on me. For a long time, father, brother-in-law and son had made Leicester Square, and the surroundings streets of Soho, their home. Because all three had dogs, they could never get a proper place at a shelter. I looked forward to meeting Sean – the third member of this family trinity – and his dog in person.

CHAPTER 7

Dash to Hackney Wick

The walls and buildings outside Hackney Wick station were covered with amazing street art and colourful graffiti. It wasn't a place that I was overfamiliar with, but the area looked nice, trendy and up-and-coming. This part of London's East End had seen massive changes in just a few decades: one of those traditionally poor, working-class areas that had now morphed into a sought-after neighbourhood, with professionals and young people buying up flats and apartments like there was no tomorrow. There was evidence of prosperity in every Sold and Let sign.

Pulling up outside the station, I looked around. Over by the entrance, I could see a spot where I could imagine the man and his dog had been sitting. I knew he had been bedding down outside the station, and that the lady who had reached out to me on Facebook lived very close. There were a few other rough-sleepers around, and I thought I recognised one or two.

Walking across to the converted warehouse opposite, I buzzed the intercom and waited. The building was typical of the regrowth seen in the East End; wealthy young graduates settling in and changing the demographics of the area. It was good to see fresh life being breathed into the place, but I couldn't help contrasting it with the world that I inhabited. It seemed like so many people were moving forwards, getting on with their lives, having families, starting businesses and owning their own homes, all just yards away from lives filled with destitution, poverty and want.

'Hi, you must be Michelle?' The woman at the door smiled, holding out her hand. 'I'm Helen.' She had a kind face and a warm smile, framed by a gorgeous flock of flame-coloured tousled locks.

'Hi there. Yes, I am,' I said. 'Thanks for reaching out to us.'

'It's no problem,' she replied. 'Come on in, I'll introduce you to Kaizer.'

Then, as soon as she opened the door fully, I was pounced on by the most beautiful, playful, light-brown Staffie-Ridgeback cross. 'Hello there,' I said, giving him a big cuddle. 'You must be Kaizer?'

He was stunning, so spirited and full of life. Often when I am going out to collect a dog, I don't know what to expect. Although I have a way with animals, I am always conscious that when I meet a dog, it is not usually under happy circumstances, and just like humans, they can lash out when they have been traumatised or subjected to injury or anxiety. But Kaizer was the kind of dog who would lick you to death; so lovely and bright, his love of life shone through his distress, and I fell in love with him instantly.

'As you can see, he is a very friendly pup!' Helen laughed as Kaizer dashed between the two of us. 'He hasn't got a nasty bone in his body.'

'Oh yes, he's lovely.' I smiled. 'So, tell me what happened.'

Helen told me she was a busy professional who commuted into the West End daily for her job in publishing. She and her partner, Tom, had lived in the converted warehouse for a few years. Every day, she left the apartment and walked across to the station, and as she got to know people in the local area, she started noticing a homeless man and his dog in the same spot each time she passed. Eventually, she got talking to him, and over the months, they became friends.

'His name is Arthur,' she said. 'But his real name is Arturas Dumbliauskas. He's originally from Lithuania'.

'What happened to him?' I asked.

'Every morning I stop and say hello to Arthur and Kaizer on my way to work,' she said. 'I buy him a coffee and sandwich or whatever. He sells the *Big Issue*, so when a new one comes out, I buy a copy, which I read on the train.

'As the weeks and months passed, he became part of the daily make up of the area and I found myself looking forward to seeing him. He would always be there with his dog, selling his magazines near to the exit of the station. When we first met he had a much older dog but sadly he passed away. He's had Kaizer since he was a little puppy.

'One evening, I bumped into him on the train. Clearly upset and tearful, he told me that someone had vomited all over his new stack of magazines, and he was panic-stricken at the thought of not having any money for food for his dog, Kaizer. Like most people these days, I had no cash on me, so we walked over to the corner shop together to buy him some food and essentials, paying with my card. He got some bits and pieces for himself, but all he really wanted was the meatballs he uses to feed Kaizer. Arthur would always prioritise his dog over himself, making sure he was well fed and cared for.'

Clearly, Helen had become attached to Arthur and Kaizer, and a friendship had developed; I could see she genuinely cared. While Arthur was not one of my clients, I could tell from what she was saying that he fitted into a recognised pattern of despair. And even though he seemed to be a happy soul, always ready with a smile and a kind word, it seemed to me that he was very much one of the underclass, who found it difficult to get a foothold on anything resembling self-reliance. He needed support.

'Did you know where he was sleeping?' I asked. 'Did he have access to any hostels or shelters of any sort? Or did he ever talk about any family or friends? Did he always stay in the local area? Did you ever see him with friends or other homeless people?'

'At the time, he was squatting in an old, run-down, abandoned pub next to the station. There were often other people squatting there, but they never seemed to stick around for very long and seemed to be just passing through. Occasionally I would see him and his dog, sunning themselves on the roof as my train pulled into the station. They looked so comical sunbathing on the roof of a dilapidated building against a backdrop of urban sprawl!

'He did tell me he had a wife and two children back home in Lithuania. And I do recall him telling me that his son had travelled to London looking for work a few years ago. They met up, but it didn't work out. I think too much had happened between the two of them, and they never saw each other again.

'Both my partner Tom and I would always keep an eye on Arthur, and we would often get him things as and when he needed them, though he was really reluctant to accept any kind of help. Despite this, if we were ever having a barbecue or if we had made too much food, I would always make up a plate for Arthur and take it over to him. I practically had to force him to take it, as he is a very proud man and didn't like any sort of fuss or getting something for nothing.

'Even though Arthur knew where we lived and that we had offered to help him many times, he never came to bother us and would never ask us for anything, so that's why on the days leading up to the last bank holiday weekend in May, it was so unusual that he knocked on our door to ask if he could use our bathroom. He did this for a few days in a row. I was quite surprised, but happy to help him out. Then one Friday evening, we were having a party and Arthur buzzed up to ask if he could use our bathroom again. As soon as he came up, Tom noticed straight away that he was really struggling. He was clearly in a great deal of pain.

'He didn't look at all well, but still insisted that he just had a bit of a tummy bug. I asked him if there was anything I could do for him, but he said he would be fine and that he'd faced far worse in his years living rough. Later that evening, I went out to check on him a few times, as I was concerned and I couldn't stop thinking about him. But again, he told me he was fine, coping OK, and that I really shouldn't worry about him. I just had a nagging feeling inside that something was not quite as it should be.'

'We all have to trust our instincts,' I told her. 'Sometimes people are actually not fully aware of their own illnesses or conditions. What happened next?'

'An hour or so later,' said Helen, 'the intercom buzzed again. As soon as I answered I could hear Kaizer barking and Arthur's frail voice begging for help. I raced across, and there he was in a terrible state on the doorstep. Kaizer was beside himself, licking and nudging him with his nose. Tom and I calmed him down and gave Kaizer some water to drink. Arthur was so panicked – I could see the fear in his eyes – but his first and only concern was for his dog. He was adamant he didn't want to cause a fuss, but we called an ambulance. The rain was bucketing down, and he refused to come inside at first, so we sat outside with him, trying to stay out of the rain and talking to him. He was terrified about Kaizer and what would become of him, and who would look after him in the event of something happening to him.

'Tom told him we would, of course, take care of Kaizer, and that he was not to worry at all about him. We waited and waited, and I could see that Arthur was getting worse as the time dragged on. We had been outside in the rain for ages when he finally agreed to come inside, while Tom called the ambulance service again to complain about the length of time they were taking. We were really worried about him.'

'Was he conscious at that point?' I asked, sipping the cup of tea she had handed me.

'He was, but not fully compos mentis,' she said. 'He was drifting in and out and mumbling about Kaizer as we helped him inside. Three hours after we called them, the ambulance service finally arrived. Amazingly, we then had a kind of stand-off where both paramedics scratched their chins, trying to decide what to do with Arthur.'

Through years of experience with similar circumstances, I knew what Helen was about to say. It's an old problem when it comes to rough-sleepers and their dogs. For obvious reasons, the emergency services cannot take their animals, and there is nowhere for them to go. This is the central thrust of Dogs on the Streets – we exist for just this reason.

'I didn't know what to do,' said Helen. I could see her getting visibly distressed as she relived the moment Arthur was collapsing in her living room.

'Arthur begged the paramedics to let his dog go with him, and even refused to get in the ambulance. We could all see he was gravely ill; his face was pallid and grey; he was clutching his stomach as if he had been stabbed. Something had to be done, and straight away. In the end, I persuaded him to let the ambulance service take him to hospital without Kaizer. But he made me promise I'd look after his dog and make sure he was safe. It was so upsetting. Tom began to lose his temper and practically had to force the paramedics to take the situation seriously and recognise how much pain he was clearly in. They finally took him in the early hours of the morning.'

In my experience, many of the emergency services were reluctant to take homeless people, as they were viewed as worthless drug addicts, off their heads on spice.

'Kaizer is still quite a young puppy – I think Arthur said he's about a year old – and he was clearly fretting.

Tom ended up sleeping in our living room with him, as this was his first time not sleeping outside and without Arthur, who at that time had been living in a tent under a flyover. We then had the problem of not knowing where they had taken Arthur. I didn't realise that Arthur wasn't his given name up to this point, and we had no idea what his surname was. We didn't know how long he might be gone, and now we had this big puppy in our small, flat. I reached out on the Locals Facebook group, and that's how we found you, Michelle.'

While I had come across very similar situations many times before, it was no less upsetting. Arthur was a stranger in a foreign land, miles from home, with no family or friends, no roof over his head and no way to survive without a helping hand. The scale of the problems faced by homeless people really hits home when a catastrophe like this happens. It is the people around us, our loved ones, whom we all rely on to take care of us in times of trouble. But for one reason or another, some of us find themselves cast adrift without an anchor – and with no safety net.

Helen was clearly deeply upset by what had happened. She told me she had cried her eyes out as she watched the ambulance speed off through the traffic, blue lights flashing and sirens blasting out into the night. A solitary tear trickled down her cheek as she spoke.

'I'd hate myself if Kaizer got lost in the system,' she said. 'I couldn't bear the thought of him being locked up in a dog pound, labelled as a number, far away from Arthur and with nobody to make sure they were reunited. I called all sorts of places – the council, the RSPCA, the police – but I was frantic in case he got lost in the big machine and Arthur would never be able to find him.'

'That can happen, I'm afraid,' I told her. 'You did the right thing.'

'I read your website and had no hesitation in messaging you. I think what you do is wonderful.'

'Thank you, you're very kind.' I smiled. 'It is a labour of love, but I am part of a big team. We've gone from strength to strength over the past few years. There are good people out there who want to help.

'Where is Arthur now?' I asked her.

'They took him to Homerton Hospital,' Helen said. 'As soon as I have Kaizer settled, I'll go straight there and reassure Arthur that his best friend is perfectly safe and well with us. He can stay for as long as necessary until Arthur is on the mend. We have a beautiful kennel for him to settle into and where he will have everything he needs until Arthur is well enough to come and collect him. After that, we will support him.'

'Thank you, Michelle,' Helen said. 'You're an angel.'

Kaizer happily came along with me and sat on the back seat of my little black Fiesta, watching the world go by as I drove out to his new temporary home at the emergency kennels we used.

For those seeking to support and find accommodation for homeless individuals, it is a lot harder to get them through the pathway when they have dogs. And when people like Arthur go into the hospital and we look after their dogs at the emergency kennels, it is then hard to find accommodation where they can convalesce that will also accept their dogs. In a housing market increasingly dominated by rental properties, private landlords have to start accepting dogs. Most reluctance to allow dogs is grounded in perceptions of animals as anti social creatures. Clearly, when pet dogs are regularly left alone for long periods of time, they can often develop destructive tendencies and neurosis through lack of socialisation and exercise, but landlords are unlikely to experience these sorts of problems with dogs who have lived among the homeless community. These animals, used to being outdoors a lot more of the time, walking and being around strangers, tend to have far fewer behavioural issues than home-reared pet dogs. Street dogs are very sociable and are comfortable interacting with groups of different people all the time. When people go into accommodation after coming off the streets, their dogs are usually far better behaved than their traditionally domesticated counterparts. Moreover, if and when tenants, for whatever reason, leave that property, their dogs always go with them and are never left behind or abandoned. We need to get this message across, not just to private landlords, but to health-care providers, too.

Please Don't Leave Me

CHAPTER 8

Mobile Love

Sunday has always been a busy day for me. On top of the daily barrage of emails and overnight messages, feeding my own menagerie and getting my family up and moving, there is the added responsibility of driving the mobile vet station from The Sanctuary into Central London. Without a doubt, this mobile clinic is our greatest innovation. Poppy made me realise that I had to take to the streets and take a hands-on, pre-emptive approach in order to reach the desolate souls scattered across London. It is just not enough to offer support or make it available; in order to make any real difference, services have to be taken to those in need of them. Of course, none of this would have been possible without the kindness of strangers. One of those strangers was a wonderful man: a very wealthy and successful businessman who commuted regularly to his office in the city. On his commute, he would often stop and say hello to one of my clients, Brian, seated in his usual spot with his three little dogs on the concourse outside Euston station. Over the weeks and months, Brian and his new friend got to know each other, and Brian told him all about how he came to be homeless. When the man asked Brian how he managed with his dogs, he told him about me and Dogs on the Streets.

Completely out of the blue, I then got a call from our wonderful benefactor, saying he wanted to offer his help and support. He ended up buying us a brand-new van, but not stopping at that, he got the whole thing customised and kitted out with hot running water, electricity and a vet's treatment table. He also funded countless medicines, vaccines and everything we would need to care for our clients' dogs. He even paid for a very talented man to spray-paint our DOTS logo right across the side of our big white battle bus!

Word seemed to spread like wildfire, as if we had moved up a gear, which of course we had. With the new battle bus, I felt invigorated, ready to take on the world, and eager to immerse myself in a life spent helping the helpless. Soon, more and more people came out of the woodwork to offer their services. Just like me, they could see what was happening all around us, that the problem was getting worse, not better, and more and more people were finding themselves on the streets after their lives had broken down. It can be such a daunting task, going from wanting to help the homeless and their dogs to actually getting up and doing something about it. With our new fully equipped mobile vet station, I had the perfect vehicle to motivate the people who wanted to help to get off their sofas and out onto the streets, where they can make a real difference. The van was impressive: huge, beautiful, and with its brightly coloured DOTS logo, it stood out, not only on the busy streets of the capital, but also on social media. Within days of posting appeals for volunteers, we started getting highly qualified vets keen to help and offering their services for free.

Kylie Simons responded to a Facebook post I made. we instantly hit it off; she is a Londoner, born and brought up in the city. Like so many others, she had witnessed first-hand the explosion in the homeless population. I could tell straight away that Kylie was most definitely the genuine article: she is a dedicated vet, a highly trained and experienced animal medic with a fantastic career, but more importantly, she has a massive heart. From the moment she messaged me, I knew she was exactly the kind of person that we so desperately needed.

Her first day on the mobile vet station was a real baptism of fire; we were so busy that day. Kylie turned up bright and early, raring to go. Little did she know that the other vet hadn't been able to make it, leaving her to man the fort alone. But like the true professional she is, she had the place battened down and shipshape within minutes of her arrival.

During a rare quiet point in the day, she told me how she had wanted to work with animals from a very early age.

'Ever since I was a little girl, I have always wanted to be a vet,' she said, as we grabbed a cheeky coffee at the back of the van. 'I just love being around animals, and I have never known anything different.

'The unconditional love and loyalty an animal can give a person is second to none. I have a cat called Meme, and Charlie, a retired racehorse. They really are part of my close family and I love them dearly. I know only too well the benefits of having a pet, but the bond between the home-less clients and their dogs that I have seen here today gives that relationship a new, greater meaning for me.'

She spoke with kind eyes and a bright smile, but her words were tinged with a bittersweet sadness. Years of witnessing the emotional ties that rough-sleepers have with their animals never fails to move me. And while I knew Kylie had experienced so much already during her career and saved countless animals, I knew that today she had recognised the sense of belonging that an animal can give to a person who has nothing else in their lives but the love of their dogs.

'A lot of the owners who have brought their dogs here today need nothing more than encouragement and support; somebody like me to reassure them that they are doing a good job and that their animals are well cared for,' she said. 'Every person I have seen here today had genuine love and concern for their best friend's welfare. In most cases, it was plain to see that they put their dog's health and safety above their own.

'When I was a kid, I felt so lucky that I had the opportunity to work at my local stables, and I even went to stay on farms in my school holidays, just to be around animals and to get the experience I craved. Then I was accepted to the Royal Veterinary College for vet training and graduated in 2008. After graduating I travelled and volunteered at the Esther Honey Foundation, which is a world-renowned non-profit veterinary practice in the Cook Islands in the South Pacific.

'On returning to the UK, I started my first job in a small animal clinic in Surrey. I was there for three years before deciding to move more into the charity sector, and I started working at the Celia Hammond Animal Trust, a London-based charity dedicated to the rescue and homing of abandoned cats, dogs and other pets.

'After eighteen months as the head vet at Celia Hammond, I then left to set up my own clinic as a low-cost referral centre in 2014. Which is where I am now. I think it's essential and almost a duty to put my skills to good use. and I try very hard to do a mix of first-opinion work, whereby I would be the first vet to examine an animal and offer a diagnosis, and also charity, breeding and referral work.

'Growing up and then living in London, I had always been acutely aware of the homelessness problem, and it had always bothered me, but I felt powerless to do anything about it. In more recent years it seemed to be getting worse, not better, with more and more people sleeping rough. I had started to look into possible ways to volunteer, and then I saw your Facebook post, Michelle. You were appealing for vet volunteers for your Dogs on the Streets charity, so here I am!'

'Well, I am very happy to have you on board, Kylie.' I beamed. 'Thank you ever so much. How have you found your first day?'

'This is the first time I've done anything remotely like mobile vetting,' she said. 'I was tentative at first, but your whole team has been so fantastic. And the van's amazing – it's so well-equipped, you've really thought of everything! Which is just as well, given how busy we've been today.

'It's impossible not to notice how all the clients and their dogs are so well bonded and really well behaved. Most pets are kept in a house all day while their owners are out at work, or at college or school. Being cooped up all day, while often unavoidable, isn't good for them. But street dogs are out in the open all day and interact with all sorts of people of different shapes and sizes; they are around traffic noise and the hustle and bustle of the city. They become socialised and less prone to trauma. In fact, as whole, they behave a lot better than most of the dogs I come across at my practice!

'As well as giving preventative care and treating any medical conditions or injuries, I feel like a lot of the time my job was to reassure clients that their dogs are healthy and well looked after. You can tell how much they love their dogs and are worried for them, and me being able to give them a check-over and provide that reassurance is a great comfort to them.

'At the moment, I can do one mobile vet station shift per month, but I would very much like to expand on that and do whatever I can to help.'

'Well, we are always looking for an extra pair of hands,' I said, not passing up an opportunity. 'We get out into the streets of London regularly with bags full of food, doggie accessories, socks and hot drinks. You are more than welcome anytime during the weekday evenings.'

'That sounds great, Michelle,' she said. 'I'd love to. Your dedication to the dogs and your clients is never-ending. Do you ever get a day off?'

'Ha ha! Chance would be a fine thing!' I laughed.

More and more vets like Kylie, and veterinary assistants with experience, started volunteering at the new mobile surgery, and in no time at all, the whole thing developed into the shining beacon of light it is now. In addition to the highly trained and skilled veterinary surgeons who give up their time for nothing, selfless volunteers offer their time to drive vans and to fetch and carry things, as well just helping those in need.

To top it all, Fiona, who grooms my own dogs, offered her services completely free of charge. On the last Sunday of every month, she began parking up behind our vet station in order to treat all the street dogs to a thorough sprucing up in her mobile grooming vehicle. They went in looking sad, forlorn, dirty and dishevelled, like they'd been dragged through a hedge backwards, and came out sparkling, full of zest, looking brand spanking new and ready for the catwalks! It really was a sight for sore eyes. Her big, blustering, booming, bright blue beauty salon burst onto the streets of London. 'Fee's Pamper Camper' is now a regular sight, and a bit of colourful tourist attraction to boot!

Our mobile vet station gives our clients easy access to pre-vet care and professional medical help and support, as well as providing food, flea collars, toys and anything that a dog might need to thrive. We park up every Sunday on one of London's busiest streets, The Strand, opposite the police station at Charing Cross.

'Hello David.' I smiled as a familiar face boarded the station. 'How are you today?'

'Fine thanks, Michelle,' he mumbled, pulling out his ever-present notebook, a tiny betting-shop pen attached to it with a piece of ragged string and some sticky tape. He and Mr J were regular visitors to us. News travels incredibly fast around the homeless community, and as soon as he'd heard about our services, David had brought Mr J along for a check-up and to get him up to date with all his jabs, then treated him to a bath and pamper session at Fee's Pamper Camper.

'And how are you, Mr J?' I asked, lifting his little Jack Russell Terrier onto the treatment table.

Looking up with a worried frown on his face, David flicked through the pages of his notebook. 'He is up to date with all his vaccinations and jabs now,' he stuttered.

'But the castration today . . . I have to say, I'm concerned about Mr J having a general anaesthetic for this.'

'You have nothing to worry about, David,' our vet assured him, filling up the syringe and squeezing out the excess trapped air.

Softly stroking Mr J, I smiled at him as he succumbed to the sedation and slowly closed his eyes, falling fast asleep. David kept a careful log of every one of the preventative treatments and procedures his beloved dog had been given. It was all carefully recorded, along with all the dog's future appointments, in the little black notebook he kept in his inside breast pocket. Castration is a serious operation by any standards; I could see that David was worried sick, so I did my level best to reassure him.

The two of them were a familiar sight on the streets of the West End, and David could often be seen walking around with his head in the clouds, his little dog balanced precariously on his shoulders. Meticulous by nature, David cared for Mr J with the passion and care of a dedicated father and the slide-rule accuracy of his time-served profession as an architect. I have always been careful never to pry too much into our clients' lives and their stories; I think it's much less intrusive to allow people to open up in their own time. If they wanted to share their stories of what had happened to them and how they ended up destitute, I was always ready to listen, but this had to be in their own time and on their own terms. David's story, which he had shared with me some years back, a few weeks after he first started bringing Mr J to see us, was particularly poignant.

'You know, Michelle, I used to be *alive*,' he had told me. 'I had a beautiful wife and a gorgeous daughter. She was only six years old.' David was a very softly spoken, clearly well-educated man with a cultured accent and a broad vocabulary. His clothes were understandably worn and tatty, but there was a natural elegance about him.

'What happened, David?' I smiled warmly, resting my hand on his forearm. 'You can tell me, but only if you want to.'

He looked exhausted, puffed and worn from years spent trudging the streets out in the cold.

'I'd like to, Michelle,' he said. 'I spend my days walking around, but I plot no course and I don't travel from one place to another; for me, there is no destination, just a journey with little or no point or purpose to it, or anything else that I can see. I shuffle through the days on autopilot, like a zombie not going anywhere, just walking.

'But my life once seemed so complete: a loving family, a nice house, a good job, holidays abroad and plenty of friends and kindness around me. I'd always had a love of buildings and studied for years, following my dream to become an architect – which I now think of as ironic when I traipse past some of the finest architecture in the world. But it all goes unnoticed, lost to me as no more than a pale reflection of my former life, of who I used to be.'

'Where are you from, David?' I asked gently. 'Where was your home and what happened?'

With tears streaming down his face into his greying, straggly beard, he sat with his head bowed, staring at the floor. He told me that he and his wife had tried for some years to have a baby. Finally, she fell pregnant, and they were both over the moon. She gave birth to a healthy little girl, and they settled down to family life in a quiet, leafy corner of semi-rural Surrey. David had a successful career as an architect, and his wife gave up her job as a teacher to become a stay-at-home mum. One Christmas, they bought their little girl a Jack Russell Terrier, whom she called Mr J. David told me how his daughter doted on the puppy and couldn't wait to take him out on walks. Then, with the pup no more than a few weeks old, his wife and daughter went away for the weekend to visit relatives. The puppy was too young to travel, so they had agreed that David would stay at home to look after him. The following night, two police officers called at his home and gave him the devastating news that his wife and daughter had been involved in an horrific car crash. They had both been killed. He was consumed with an overwhelming sadness so big he could not see his way out of it. He was beyond reach.

'From that point on, everything has happened in a blur,' he sobbed. 'I have a vague memory of sitting in the church at their funeral, but it feels as though that person was somebody else. People spoke to me, but I couldn't hear their words, and my whole being became an echo of the past. In the days after the burial, the house was full of people mourning the death of my wife and child, but I was completely numb. I felt nothing at all. Eventually, everybody drifted away and I was alone. Just me and my little girl's puppy, Mr J. The silence in the house was deafening.

'I could hardly get out of bed, and just stared at the ceiling for endless hours. Whenever I did drop off to sleep, it was only for the briefest of moments, and my wife and daughter would appear, smiling and laughing in my dreams. Then, when I awoke, the reality and the sheer dread of the day ahead struck me all over again and my body felt as though it been hit by an express train. I felt paralysed and found myself unable to move, frozen and rooted in the horror of that terrible moment when I was told about the crash. I closed down, unable to work, just simply existing. Ultimately, I lost my job, the letters and the bills piled up behind the front door, and I imploded. I couldn't see a way out.'

David told me how the pressure inside him built and built, until one day, he put Mr J's lead on, opened the front door of their neat three-bedroom semi, and just walked out: as simple as that. He left his life behind and took nothing with him but the clothes he was wearing. The two just walked and walked, for mile after mile, without looking back. Years later, they are still walking aimlessly around the streets of London. And then one day, completely out of the blue, David and Mr J walked into the mobile vet station on The Strand, and they have been a part of my life ever since.

CHAPTER 9

Meeting Arthur

With Kaizer safely settled in at The Sanctuary, I jumped into my little car and dashed back to the East End. Thankfully, the traffic was pretty forgiving, and I got through Stratford and Hackney to Homerton Hospital in no time at all. I couldn't quite put my finger on it, but I had a funny feeling about Arthur Dumbliauskas. While he had never been one of my clients, I found myself thinking about him and Kaizer a lot. Meeting Helen and listening to her talk, I'd built up a picture of a kind and soulful man who not only loved his dog but also cared about people. It's odd how individuals link or connect with strangers, and how some ideas become lodged in your mind. I had a feeling as I walked into the hospital foyer that there was a special journey about to unfold in front of me.

I had prioritised going to the hospital to see Arthur in person, because I understood how concerned he would be about his dog. He needed to be reassured that Kaizer was safe, and that they would be reunited as soon as he was well enough. It was the least I could do. I knew before I went there that Arthur must have been in a serious condition, and I was anxious for him. Within seconds of walking onto the ward, my worst fears were confirmed. Every bed was occupied, and all of the patients were quite clearly dangerously ill.

'Hi, I'm looking for Arthur Dumbliauskas,' I said to the nurse at the desk in the middle of the ward. 'Can you tell me where I might find him?'

'Yes, of course,' she smiled. 'Are you a friend or a relative?'

Her words hit me with a grim starkness – he had no friends and no family. This man, as far as I was aware, was completely alone in the world, and had nobody – except, of course, his loving pet and life companion, Kaizer.

'Well, I'm neither really,' I told her. 'I'm a support worker for the homeless. I have Arthur's dog and I wanted to speak to him about it. Is that OK?'

'Of course it is,' she replied warmly. 'He's in the end bay, down the corridor on the right-hand side.'

Tentatively, I stepped into the bay and instantly spotted Arthur. He had a look that was all too familiar to me. It was a look that took me back to my own dark days as a teenage runaway sleeping rough under stairwells, in telephone boxes and in hospital toilets. I see it every day and spend my life helping people out of that particular mire. He was fast asleep when I arrived, so I sat patiently at his bedside and waited. His gentle snore was muffled by the constant beeping noises, hustle and bustle going on all around as he slept. He shared a bay with three other men, all of whom looked gravely ill, hooked up to serious-looking machines and monitors. I could see Arthur was at the sharp end of the hospital.

But despite the drama of the ward, I realised as I sat there that I had found myself a rare moment of calm in the midst of my hectic life. As Arthur slept, I had time to reflect on what had happened that day, and all the other days stretching back into what seemed like an endless swirling vortex of chaos, heartache and human misery. I attacked the dilemma of homelessness and lost connections with gusto and faced it head-on, day in, day out, twenty-four/ seven and all year round. Maybe throwing myself into the insurmountable was, in no small way, part of my own therapeutic process, a way to tackle the traumas that had, at times, threatened to blight my own existence. Certainly, I knew in some small way what it felt like to be trudging around the city at night without any direction or focus. Running away from the burden of sadness and despair, I had found solace in the potentially precarious world of London's night-time economy and, of course, John and the travelling fairground. I knew from my own experiences how hard it can be facing life alone in dark places, with nobody to hold your hand and tell you everything is going to be OK.

Of course, it isn't going to be OK, and never will be, unless these complex issues can be tackled. Sitting there watching Arthur, I thought of all the people who have chipped in and altruistically volunteered their services to Dogs on the Streets and similar services. I reflected on the importance of caring for the vulnerable, and how putting something back into a society that sometimes appears as if it doesn't care is actually really valuable, rewarding and beneficial. Poppy's legacy was alive and well.

Arthur's face was an orange-yellow colour and looked very pallid. I tried to imagine what he been through, where he had come from and what his story was. His face was long and drawn, weathered and craggy, with closely cropped hair, tattoos and heavy earrings that had stretched and elongated his earlobes.

'Hi there,' I said softly, smiling, as he opened his eyes. 'How are you feeling today?'

'Thank you,' he said meekly, 'I am OK. Are you a nurse or doctor?'

'No, Arthur,' I replied. 'I'm called Michelle Clark, and like you, I'm an animal lover.'

'Kaizer!' he said sharply, trying to sit up. 'Where is Kaizer? Is he OK? Where have they taken him?'

The very mention of his dog sparked Arthur into life. Straight away, his first thoughts were for him. He was very confused, still half-asleep, and perhaps groggy from all the medication he'd been given.

'He's perfectly fine,' I told him reassuringly, reaching out to hold his hand as I did so. 'Kaizer is safe and well, Arthur. You have my word.' Taking out my phone, I showed him a couple of photos of Kaizer that I'd taken at The Sanctuary. Tears streamed down Arthur's face as he took hold of the phone in both hands and gazed at his beloved pooch. 'You see,' I said. 'He's happy and being well cared for by us.'

'Thank you, thank you,' he sobbed. 'I have been worried sick about him. We are all each other has in the world. I could not bear the thought of something bad happening to him or him getting lost, out there all on his own.'

'Well, he's not,' I said, reassuringly. 'He is happy, healthy and well fed. And he'll be waiting for you to come and get him, just as soon as you're better.'

'But who are you?' he pleaded. 'I am sorry to ask – are you a hospital worker, social services, or something like that?'

'No, I run a charity called Dogs on the Streets. We look after the needs of homeless people and their dogs.'

'There are many homeless people with dogs in London,' he said. 'I have heard about you and your vehicle on The Strand, but never thought to come and see you. How did you know about me and Kaizer? Did the ambulance people tell you?'

'No, it was Helen,' I told him. 'The lady who lives across the street from your pitch outside the station. Do you remember knocking on her door late at night when you fell ill?'

'Yes, of course, Helen,' he said, trying to smile. 'She is so nice, and stops to chat to me every day, sometimes a few times a day. She always buys a *Big Issue* from me and brings me food and hot drinks. She is a very kind woman. And Tom is a very nice and kind man.'

'What happened, Arthur?' I asked gently. 'How long have you been ill and in pain?'

'It started a month or two ago,' he told me. 'I had a pain in my back that wouldn't go away. I went to a medical centre and they gave me some tablets, but they didn't really help. I thought if I took my mind off it, the pain would eventually go away.

'Then the pain spread to my stomach, and I found it very hard to go to the toilet. Then when I did, it was so painful to go and then diarrhoea followed, and I struggled to find a toilet that I could use. I gritted my teeth and just battled through the day. Night times were always bad, and I struggled to eat or sleep. My clothes started to feel baggy, and I knew I was losing weight very rapidly.'

'Why didn't you get some help at that stage, Arthur?' I asked.

'To be honest, nobody cares about people like me. Most just walk past without even looking at me, as if I am invisible. This is the same for many homeless people. We go unnoticed.'

'But there are kind people out there who want to help,' I told him. 'There is always some help available, especially if you are sick.'

'Not everybody is kind like Helen and Tom, and you, of course, Michelle,' he replied. 'Sometimes I feel like a statue that no one wants to look at. Like I don't exist.'

Nobody ever plans on being homeless, and nobody ever picks it as a lifestyle choice. Homelessness for Arthur came at the end of a despairing slide into a dysfunctional way of life that fate propelled him into. He paid the price for the bad choices he made as he became increasingly alienated from everything he knew after losing his job as an electrician. Falling behind with his rent and being unable to support his young family, Arthur couldn't bear the evidence of what he saw as his 'failure', and turned his rage at himself outwards. Furious rows with his wife followed, and they must have been very frightening for her and their child, often ending with him breaking things and slamming doors before disappearing for hours, sometimes days, at a time. Despite his obvious unhappiness at what was clearly a very difficult time for all, he told me that his world fell apart completely in the aftermath of the chaotic break-up with his wife.

Although it took place in Arthur's home city of Vilnius, the capital of Lithuania, the path Arthur fell onto was a familiar one, replicated in towns and cities throughout the world. Roaming the building sites and factories around the city looking for work, he had his first taste of drifting aimlessly without anyone or anything to show him the way. Almost inevitably, he fell in with the wrong types of people and started taking drugs. Predictably, a life of petty crime followed, as he became more and more embroiled in street gangs and organised crime.

Vilnius offered little chance of escape from the lifestyle Arthur had become caught up in. Although entirely different from the UK in terms of culture, outlook and history, it was just another small city surviving in a sea of change that engulfed the whole of the former Soviet Union and Eastern Europe. Huge swathes of people were displaced and became lost in the massive upheaval and dramatic changes that followed the collapse of communism. Vilnius could be a harsh and unforgiving place, with little or no safety net to catch people when they fell.

Like many Eastern European people in his situation, in a brave bid to turn things around, Arthur came to London, looking for work. He was arrested after crossing the Channel without a passport and thrown into a refugee camp in Kent. He stayed there for nearly a year before a political pressure group forced the release of him and others through the UK courts. Travelling to London, he toured the building sites of the capital, but just as in Lithuania, he had no luck in finding meaningful work. With nowhere to stay, he began sleeping in parks and down alleyways. In a matter of days, the last of his money ran out and he slid into a hopeless cycle of despair, begging for money to buy food by day and hiding from muggers and violent thieves by night. He ended up trapped on a treadmill of homelessness and poverty with cheap street drugs his only release. He had nobody in his life and then he met Kaizer. The two lived in and around the streets of Hackney, and Arthur took a big step forward when he became a vendor for the *Big Issue,* selling copies from his pitch outside Hackney Wick station.

He looked so sad and lost in that hospital bed. He was a quietly spoken man, and I found him to be a sensitive and kind-hearted soul; my heart bled for him. Checking his little bedside cupboard, I saw that Arthur had no possessions – nothing at all. The day after admission, he was still wearing a standard hospital-issue gown.

'Arthur, I'm going to pop out to the shops and get you a few bits to help you through your stay,' I told him, standing and grabbing my coat. 'I won't be long, I promise.' Dashing over to the retail park nearby, I raced around a supermarket like mad woman, throwing things into the basket as I went. Out of my own pocket, I bought him a couple of pairs of pyjamas, a dressing gown and slippers, a toothbrush, toothpaste and soap, as well as some fresh fruit, snacks and drinks. To help him stay in touch and able to check on Kaizer, I bought him a pay-as-you-go mobile phone, and added the freephone number for Dogs on the Streets to the contacts list.

Making my way back to Homerton Hospital, I dashed up to the ward and packed away his new things in his cupboard and bedside table.

'I have to go now, I'm afraid, Arthur,' I told him. 'There are some things here to keep you going, and a mobile with my number saved. Call me if you need anything, or if I can help in any way.'

'Thank you, Michelle,' he said, with tears welling in his puffy eyes. 'This is very kind of you.'

'I will be back tomorrow to check on you and say hello,' I said. 'Get some rest and I will see you soon. Take care.' Once I was back in my car, I rested my head on the steering wheel and shed a tear.

CHAPTER 10

Liam and Rosey

In the week that followed, I called into Homerton Hospital every day in order to check on Arthur and to spend some time chatting and keeping him company. People have value, no matter where they come from or what has happened to them. If any was needed, meeting Arthur provided me with a very stark but vital reminder of the importance of the inclusivity ethos that underpins everything that Dogs on the Streets does. The embodiment of this is perhaps most plainly visible in the absolute dedication of our wonderful staff and volunteers.

Along with the mobile vet station, the team is one of my proudest achievements. We are so lucky to have a wide network of independent boarding facilities, kennels and foster families ready to take in dogs in any kind of emergency. This allows us to offer respite and care when things go wrong. Street dogs can find themselves in real trouble if their owners pass away, become too ill to care for them, or become otherwise separated from their pets. The police and other agencies will often bring dogs to me to care for, knowing that they will be well looked after and either patched up, brought back to health and returned to their owners, or rehomed with a loving and attentive family or a suitable new owner.

The range of facilities we are able to provide has got better and better as we have grown, but it is the wonderful people who staff it who are the lifeblood of our organisation. They lie at the heart of the services we offer. This includes therapy sessions for dogs who have suffered trauma or loss. Astonishing though this might sound, the soft, warm tone of our dog therapist's voice as she sits reading aloud to each group of dogs has a visibly calming influence. This initiative helps them settle down and seems to allay any fears or separation anxiety they have. It really is a sight to behold! We also have an enrichment coordinator, who uses her amazing abilities to play with the dogs and stimulate their senses with carefully thought-out toys.

People and their dogs come and go all the time. Looking around the place fills me with a sense of hope that there is good in the world and people really do care. It is a privilege to start my working day from there.

I was happy that Kaizer was safe and content in his new environment, but from the moment I opened my eyes in the morning following my first visit to the hospital, I found myself thinking and worrying about Arthur. His vulnerabilities and his genuine nature shone through, and I was determined to make him feel as safe and comfortable as possible. But the day ahead was a busy one, and the list of messages and jobs to sort through had grown ever longer, continuing to stack up during the time I spent in the hospital with him.

Loading up my car, I set off for my daily calls around Central London. At that time, there were three men in particular I was hoping to catch up with. I had determined to try my best to find the right accommodation for them and their dogs. On my journey, the further I went into Soho, the more people I stopped to help and supply, and the lighter my bags became. As I turned into Leicester Square, sure as day, there was young Michael and his dog, Judge, sitting in their usual spot. Another big man with huge shoulders was standing talking to him as I approached.

'Hi Michael.' I beamed. 'How are you and Judge today?' Judge jumped up and immediately started playing with me.

'As you can see, Michelle,' Michael said, laughing, 'he's on top form. This is my Uncle Sean, the fella I was telling you about.'

'Hi Sean.' I smiled, holding out my hand. 'I'm Michelle from Dogs on the Streets. I'm very pleased to finally meet you.'

'Hello Michelle,' he said. He had a deep, rasping voice with a lovely Irish lilt. 'This here is Rosey, my faithful friend and companion. So, you're the lady who runs the mobile vet station on The Strand, are you?'

'Yes,' I said. 'That's right. Have you been there? You are very welcome to bring Rosey along if she has any problems or medical issues. We would be more than happy to help you. We can also provide new leads, harnesses, food, worming, de-fleaing, warm clothing and doggie treats.'

'That's wonderful, Michelle,' he replied. 'Thank you very much.'

Sean was a very chatty and personable bloke who was more than happy to tell me his story; indeed, he really wanted to.

'I was fourteen years of age when I left Ireland and travelled to London on my own looking for work,' he told me as we sat together on one of the benches in the square. 'There was nothing left for me at home, and nobody really to care for me or to care for. So, I set off to seek my fortune with nothing more than a five-pound note in my pocket and the clothes I stood up in. Unfortunately, it didn't work out too well. So many people had told me that I would find work on the building sites in and around London, but whenever I turned up looking to be taken on, I was knocked back. I ended up sleeping in the park or on benches. That's how I came to have my first dog.'

'Is that how you found Rosey?' I asked.

'No, I'm fifty-four years old, and that was almost forty years ago. My dog back then was a little stray terrier I befriended in the park. I made sure he was well looked after and watered. When you sleep rough, there are always people who will try to rob you while you're out for the count, and my little dog, Slayer, would start yapping as soon as anyone got too close to me. He was like my personal alarm! We travelled around London and the south-east together and had many adventures, but sadly, he got old and passed away. Then, some years later, I met this guy who asked me if I was interested in bare-knuckle fighting. It was the illegal sort that took place in warehouses and old garages. Anyway, he told me I could get two hundred pounds if I won the fight. I had nothing to lose and so decided to go for it.

'The fight took place in an abandoned dock building in the East End. Before going into the ring, I spotted this little Staffie chained up in the corner. She was lying on her side with her belly all swollen out of proportion, gasping and panting for air in the heat. She looked so helpless, and I felt dreadful seeing her there in chains. I asked what was wrong with her, and the guys who were running the show told me that she was a breeder dog, there to produce pups for the dog fighting. Anyhow, I fought a big guy with a baying crowd all around. They were all betting on the fights, shouting and screaming like wild animals; it was terrifying. Me and the other fella bashed each other up for forty-five minutes, but I eventually came out on top and won the fight. When I came to collect my winnings, I told them I didn't want them, asking if I could take the little Staffie instead. They told me she had a load of pups inside her. I told them they could have the pups, but I was taking this little dog with me. That was ten years ago, and here we are now.'

'So that little dog was Rosey?' I asked in amazement as I stroked her.

'Yes, that's how I met my little Rosey, and she has been my best friend ever since. Every day, every hour, every minute, she never leaves my side. We've had to sleep in some awful places, but we keep each other going. For example, I know that the coldest time of the day is between four and seven in the morning. That's when she cuddles into me and we keep each other warm. All we have in the world is each other, and as far as I am concerned, that's a win-win situation.

'What you do is priceless, Michelle. You lot are all angels in my book. So many of the homeless people I know also have dogs. We all need loving, and everyone needs a companion. Normal people walk past you every day as if you're invisible. But my dog will never leave me; she will sit beside me and stay there all day.'

'That's great, Sean.' I said. 'You can bring her along to the mobile vet station on Sunday if she needs anything. And how is your own health? Are you managing OK?'

'Thank you, Michelle,' he said tearfully. 'As you know, the biggest headache we all face is getting help. I can't get any because I haven't got an address or anywhere to live. Everywhere I go, say they won't take dogs. I won't leave

Rosey, I'd die first. As for my health, I'm not in the best nick these days, and I struggle to look after myself, to be honest. I've got bad arthritis and a heart problem. I'm also having problems with my memory. But my worst fear is being alone. I couldn't bear the thought of something happening to her. Without Rosey, I would be isolated and lost.'

'Well let me tell you,' I said, battling to hold back the tears myself, 'I'm going to try my level best to find you, Michael and Mick, as well as your dogs, somewhere decent to live – some proper accommodation.'

At DOTS, our ultimate goal is to make sure that the owners and their dogs stay together. Services and councils have been slow to understand that they have no right to tell someone they need to give up their dog in order to access any help. Those needing help do not need to sacrifice their dogs in order to get it. The responsibility lies with services; they must find the right accommodation for these people – and their animals. Twenty-first-century dogs are family, and this is especially true for rough sleepers. Their dogs give them a sense of purpose, helping them to get through the day. Caring for their pets is a huge responsibility and demands a consistent routine, and is something that they can really learn from. Sadly, when a person ends up out on the street, they lose control of their own life. The only thing they own and have any duty to care for is their dog. So, what right does anyone have to split them up?

There is such a bitter irony in talking to a man about how isolated and alone he is, while sitting in the middle of one of the busiest thoroughfares there is, right in the heart of one of the largest capital cities in the world, where millions of people come and go every minute of the day. It is a humbling experience.

CHAPTER 11

A Devastating Diagnosis

The ingrained sense of duty I felt for Arthur and his plight gave me a single-mindedness and made me want to focus on one specific issue in a way that I hadn't for quite some time. Even if I tried, I could never switch off from the manic hurly-burly of Dogs on the Streets. It had become the centre of my universe, and it seemed to me that I was destined to spend my life juggling and spinning many plates all at once. There was always so much to do and so many differing circumstances and back stories to explore, and so many people and dogs to accommodate and look after. As well as the daily bombardment of emails, social media posts, text messages and phone calls, there were often calls I had to take during the night that had to be followed up or actioned. Then, after feeding my own animals, I'd load up my car with all the daily goodie bags and traipse the streets of London for hours fielding a continuous avalanche of calls to my mobile all the while.

In addition to the inevitable daily demands and the far less predictable incidents that needed immediate crisis intervention, more often than not, I also had to fit in seemingly endless meetings with council staff, charities and services. Before finally reaching a decision, these groups and individuals appear content to have fifty-odd messages, two hundred emails, a meet-and-greet and a boardroom conference first! Coffee-breathed bureaucrats were the bane of my life, and I had little patience with them. I openly admit that I thoroughly deserve my reputation as a 'battleaxe'. In fact, I am quite proud of that label!!

Whenever possible, each day after dinner, I would sit down in front of a computer screen to continue the day's work. Totalling up my phone, laptop and PC, my screen time averages ten hours a day. Awareness of this, in addition to the physical and mental exhaustion I so often overrode – effectively working on willpower – really frightened the life out of me. I thought, 'Oh, my God, what am I doing? Why am I allowing this charity to overtake my life? I should be in control of the charity, not the charity in control of me.' Momentary panics like this did nothing to address the issue, though. I was on a conveyor belt fuelled by my understanding of the enormity of the homelessness problem and the specific situations of those people and their dogs, all of them so reliant on what Dogs on the Streets could provide.

Some days, it all seemed like one big car crash, with a plethora of appeals and demands flying all over the place:

meetings, people having mental health crises or addiction issues, people dealing with domestic violence, and all manner of trials and tribulations. And, of course, there were always the victims caught up in the chaos of their owners' lives – the dogs. Every individual incident needed a response, and I always felt compelled to react. Then there were the pen-pushers badgering me for facts, figures and statistics. This was particularly challenging. My clients were not numbers on a spreadsheet; they were human beings, and each week more and more of them were arriving in London, with or without dogs. I knew exactly where I wanted to direct my energy, and it wasn't in a council office. Also, despite our best efforts, for every one client we got off the streets and settled into a new home, two more would arrive.

Throughout the daily mayhem that was my life, though, I was thinking about Arthur constantly, and I refused to leave him all alone in the hospital. He had nobody, and I wanted to do everything I could to help him. He was catheterised and had only just had surgery to fit a stoma bag to alleviate the intense pressure on his bowels. Then he rang to ask me to come in early so that he had somebody with him who could help him to speak to the doctors about his condition.

That terrible moment, when his consultant told him that he had advanced pancreatic cancer and just six months to live, is burned into my memory. She just blurted it out right in front of him, without even looking at him. As I told you earlier, I was furious, and of course Arthur was devastated. His first concern – indeed, his only concern – was for Kaizer.

Afterwards, the consultant told me that she had offered him chemotherapy before, but he had turned it down because his mother had died of cancer, and he witnessed first-hand what this sort of treatment had done to her. Arthur said he wanted to live the rest of his life without the additional debilitating sickness that went with chemotherapy.

There was little or no housing provision for homeless people with a terminal illness, let alone those with a dog in tow. I was in the midst of a battle with Hackney Council to get a hostel place for Arthur and Kaizer. As I wheeled him away in his chair from the consultant's office after receiving his devastating diagnosis, he beckoned me down to his level and whispered in my ear: 'You really are my angel, Michelle.' His heartfelt words resonated deep within me, and my determination to help him wade through the mountainous wall of bureaucracy became stronger and more resolute. I decided there and then that I would move heaven and earth to make sure Arthur would get to live out his last days with his best friend Kaizer in a safe and warm environment. To help me in my fight for his rights, he officially made me his next of kin, which effectively made me his voice and strengthened my position when intervening on his behalf. Despite my best efforts, bureaucratic wheels continued to move slowly. In the meantime, I brought in fresh provisions almost every day, but having refused chemotherapy or any other sort of cancer treatment, Arthur's condition worsened.

One day, I went to visit and could see he was even more agitated than usual.

'Michelle, they say I am well enough to go home,' he said as I sat down at his bedside. 'But I told them, I have no home, and I am afraid to go out on the streets with this bag attached to my stomach.' Arthur was getting himself into a right state. Of course, he had me fighting his corner. I had been by his side every single day, and I was not about to let him down now.

'Don't worry, Arthur,' I reassured him. 'I will speak to the doctors and make them aware of the situation.'

It was clear to me, though, that an age-old prejudice was written all over this decision. I knew from all the hours I had spent on that ward that some members of staff just did not want him there. Some of them were often quite short and off-hand with Arthur, and I could tell from the way they behaved that they viewed him as having little value. He was a drug addict, a nuisance and a drain on resources. These people perceived him as taking up a bed that could be used for somebody who was, in their view, more deserving; somebody 'normal'. It was a type of discrimination that I had seen a thousand times before.

I immediately demanded a meeting with the ward manager and the hospital admin staff, telling them it was not acceptable to discharge Arthur while he was so ill.

I made them fully aware of his housing situation and told them that I was working hard to secure him a hostel place as soon as possible. I pointed out that the hospital's decision to discharge him in that state was exposing him to great risk. I argued that it was not only dangerous, but also an unnecessary threat to his well-being, to send him out onto the streets with a stoma and a catheter bag. There was no way he could keep them clean, and there was nowhere to empty or even change his bags without a serious risk of infection. Moreover, not only did putting Arthur out of the hospital endanger him, but he would also be unable to dispose of the stoma bags securely, creating a biological and public health hazard. I was adamant that, as his next of kin, I would do everything I could to block his discharge from hospital without a proper care package being put in place.

By that time, it was approaching September 2018, and Arthur had been in hospital for three months. Accepting his fate, he had refused chemotherapy after seeing what it had done to his mother; he wanted to die peacefully. It seemed, though, that because he had refused treatment, the doctors had lost interest in him, and little was offered to make him more comfortable. He was slowly deteriorating in front of me, and I just did not feel that his care was adequate. He needed better and more effective palliative provision, so I told the hospital that Arthur was refusing to leave. Eventually, they backed down and allowed him to stay until I had found suitable accommodation for him.

Winning this struggle with the hospital bigwigs had brought a temporary relief from the most immediate threat that Arthur would be put back on the streets to die, but now I had to gird my loins for the next engagement. With the battle lines drawn, I prepared myself to lock horns with Hackney Council Housing Department!

CHAPTER 12

Mobile Hate

In many ways, Arthur's experience was a wake-up call, a stark reminder of the complexity of the problems we were battling. Although the evidence of discrimination on a ward where terminally ill patients were being cared for was shocking, the attitudes highlighted by Arthur's plight were ones that I had come across many times before. A couple of years after DOTS had been set up, those who worked for the charity were still regularly confronted by the same old uninformed prejudice, rolled out and repeated over and over again. I learned very early on that not everyone shared the compassion of our volunteers, and unenlightened members of the public would often feel they had some sort of agency over us, seeming to feel compelled to point out what they viewed as the error of our ways.

I recall one man who took it upon himself to be brutally explicit about the homelessness dilemma as he saw it. Walking up to our stall at the back of the mobile vet station, he confronted us by saying, 'You people are just promoting poverty.' Our volunteers had set up the Dogs on the Streets gazebo as usual, and the tables were all laid out with new leads, harnesses, doggie treats and anything a street dog might need. 'It's not right that these people should have dogs,' he protested.

'Sir, you're making assumptions without knowing the facts,' I told him. 'We are—'

But the man just talked loudly over me, not even letting me finish my sentence.

'It's a money-making scam,' he screamed, waving his arms aggressively. 'You're all pathetic. You're allowing these poor animals to live a life of misery, trudging around the streets with the dregs of society. You're feeding a the whole thing.'

'Please calm down,' I told him. 'We are a not-for-profit—'

'It shouldn't be allowed,' he butted in again. 'You should all be locked up. It's a scam.'

The same old, tired narrow-mindedness and preconceptions had surfaced yet again. It is disheartening to see the reality of how some view the homeless. But despite his vile attack, I felt a degree of sympathy for the man. He was naive as to how and why some people's lives are turned upside down in no time at all and through no fault of their own. I knew he hadn't had the experience of talking to people on the streets, I knew he hadn't any idea of the overwhelming shadow of mental health issues, I knew he had no concept of what a street dog gives to a homeless person, and I also knew that his misplaced anger was born out of ignorance. However, I despaired at his unwillingness to listen and the sheer absence of knowledge informing his judgemental stance on both Dogs on the Streets and the issue of homelessness.

'We have to live here and run our shops and businesses with these people sleeping in our doorways and littering up the streets. They take drugs openly and shout obscenities at the people going about their day-to-day business,' he continued.

The people in the queue for the vet station were staring at him, dumbstruck. Some of the volunteers had ashen faces as they listened to the man's tirade. 'But sir . . .' One of volunteers stepped in, in an effort to defuse a situation that could easily get out of hand. 'We have to have compassion for those who struggle with life, and their dogs give them focus, something to be responsible for and a reason to live. These dogs aren't dangerous, they're timid companions who loyally stay with their owners through thick and thin.'

With no ears to hear this, our visitor sneered, 'Yeah, right.'

Undeterred, our worker continued. 'I always think that anything that makes anybody else feel less alone can only be a good thing. Don't you agree?'

'Yes, and anything that makes you people earn a few bob by abusing the Charities Act is only ever going to line your pockets. If the homeless didn't exist, you lot would be out of a job.'

'But I am a volunteer, sir,' our man said. 'I don't get paid to do this. I do it because it is the right thing to do. I have the time and the resources to help, so why shouldn't I do just that?'

'Come off it,' was the response. 'Are you seriously telling me that someone here isn't getting rich from all this? You're having a laugh, mate. Look at you all, with your logos and your posh new fleeces – who is paying for all that? You are milking the system for everything you can get. It is poverty porn, that's what it is; no more, no less. You bunch of do-gooders are all feeding off this like energy vampires. I'll tell you who is paying for this lot – me! Hard-working people like me, who pay their taxes so these scroungers and scruffs can sit around all day taking drugs and drinking cheap, extra-strength lager in full view of families out for the day or shopping.'

'We are funded by donations – we don't get any government handouts at all. You are so wrong to make these assumptions without being aware of the full facts,' I told the man. Try as I might, though, I could see that he would simply not listen to reason. There really was no telling him anything at all. Eventually, he stormed off down the street, still irate about what he thought was a money-making scheme and get-rich-quick charity fraud.

Perhaps it was something in the air that day, or a bizarre cluster of irrational coincidences, but his negativity seemed to infect the atmosphere. Out of the corner of my eye, I could see Tina, one of our regular clients, becoming more and more agitated as her allotted time slot with the vet came and went. Sitting on the pavement outside the vet station, her dog by her side, fidgeting nervously, she had heard the entire tirade of that bigot who took it upon himself to dispense his twisted logic on us all before stomping off down the road. She started stroking the dog more and more vigorously – evidence of her rising tension. I knew something could happen, so I did my best to placate her.

'It'll be fine, Tina,' I told her. 'We're rushed off our feet and just really busy today, and we're already way behind.'

'Well, this is my appointment time,' she protested, her face reddened and angry. 'This is my appointment time and I've waited in line long enough. It's not good enough. I've got things to do and places to be.'

The dispossessed have absolutely nothing to lose, and they can sometimes be volatile and unpredictable. Situations can quite easily get out of control, and the most mundane of occurrences can, so quickly and so unexpectedly, blow up into something unmanageable. Dealing with people with long, traumatic histories, who are more often than not addicted to substances, alcohol and drugs, and may also have serious mental health conditions, can be tricky. Full-scale meltdowns can inevitably follow their rising sense of abandonment and loss of connection. For most of us, the people we share our lives with, face troubles with and overcome hurdles alongside are the people who define us, engage us and make us who we are. When a homeless person loses those connections, they have nothing left and can very quickly move through their own gears and become violent and aggressive.

Tina and her mastiff, Steve, had arranged to see the vet that day, but the vet had been tied up with an emergency elsewhere, was running late and had found it impossible to arrive at The Strand on time. Very quickly, Tina's agitation turned to anger and hostility. In the blink of an eye, a seemingly innocuous situation turned volatile.

'You f***ing bitch,' she screamed at the top of her voice as she made a grab for me. 'You don't care, nobody really cares; we are just pieces of meat to you. That man was right.'

She stared into my eyes and spat in my face. I was dumbstruck. She then lunged forward, her flailing arms striking me as I tried to duck and curl up in a desperate attempt to defend myself. Steve had started barking furiously. The powder-keg atmosphere, which had begun simmering while those queueing for attention had witnessed the ferocious verbal attack directed at them and listened to unwarranted accusations hurled at those working at the station, erupted.

Tina continued lashing out and spitting at me as the rest of the team and the other homeless clients pounced, trying to hold her back. But she was like a wild banshee, intent on causing as much harm as she possibly could. It was horrendous. I didn't know what to do. I'd been attacked before, but never quite as viciously.

Others waiting to see the vet stood between us and tried to protect me. Then, in a flash, swarms of police piled out of the nearby Charing Cross police station, wrestled Tina to the ground, and quickly defused the situation. They were so professional and efficient. I don't know what might have happened without their intervention.

'Are you OK, Michelle?' one of the officers asked, putting her arm around my shoulders. 'Here, sit yourself down and have a sip of water.'

'Thank you,' I stuttered, catching my breath as I took the plastic cup. 'I'll be fine. Is Tina OK?'

When I had first met her, a few years earlier, Tina was as quiet as a mouse. Terrified and vulnerable, she seemed incapable of causing anybody any harm. We had sat in a café in Soho, and she poured out her story to me. Sheets of rain lashed the windows as she hugged her mug of hot chocolate. 'How long have you been on the streets?' I asked.

'It will be coming up to about five years, now – well, on and off,' she said. 'After my first night sleeping rough, I never imagined I would still be homeless all these years later.'

She was a good-looking woman in her mid-thirties, bright as a button with a warm smile. She had a shaved haircut with blonde and pink dye in it, and facial piercings and tattoos. Her clothes were threadbare, and her Doc Martens boots were worn and battered. Underneath the table, her bags were piled up, and Steve lay obediently on the floor next to them. The café owner knew me well and would often bend the rules to let dogs in, as long as they were well behaved and no other customers raised an objection. As ever with street dogs, Steve was no trouble at all – friendly and appreciative.

'Where are you from originally?' I asked, knowing that she wanted to tell me her story. 'Do you have any family?'

'I'm from up north,' Tina said with a pained expression. 'There is family, I suppose, but whether they are mine or not is another question.'

'How do you mean?' I asked. 'Do you not see them or have any contact with any of them?'

'No,' she said sadly. 'They all turned their backs on me. I had nowhere to go, and just ended up drifting.'

'What happened to you?' I said, placing my hand on top of hers.

'It's a long story,' she said, looking down into the steaming mug. 'Everything was fine until he moved in.'

'He?' I asked

'My so-called stepdad,' she said with a sudden look of venom in her eyes. 'And to be honest with you, Michelle, there was a time when I thought all kids went through the same as me.'

'What do you mean?' I asked.

'I was only six or seven when he started abusing me. Something inside me told me it was wrong, but at that age, it's hard to understand what's going on. Like I said, while I found it very difficult and it scared me, I thought all the kids in my street and at school went through the same thing. Like it was normal stuff, and it really didn't matter that much. It was only when I got older and started thinking about boyfriends and sex, and learning about relationships, that I realised it was all very wrong. And that the reason why I felt so bad was because I was being abused and silenced. He would come to my room at night or when nobody else was home. He jumped at every opportunity. He said that it was our little secret, and this is what parents do with their kids. He said it was natural.

'As I got older, and went to high school, I grew more and more detached. I didn't have many friends and I found myself alone a lot and easy prey for the school bullies. The kids at school used to call me names like "weirdo" and "crank", and I just didn't seem to fit in. Things got worse when I put on a bit of weight, and I started making myself sick after every mealtime. It was almost like I had some sort of release from vomiting. I know it sounds crazy, but I actually looked forward to the feeling of throwing up down the toilet. Inevitably, I then lost loads of weight and my mum started quizzing me. That was when all the arguments started.'

Blazing rows with her mother became a regular feature in Tina's world. She became increasingly withdrawn and isolated. It sounded very much as if her mother was a person who struggled with life. Tina was the youngest of seven children. Their mother had a history of violent and abusive relationships.

'Then I started hanging out with the wrong crowd,' Tina continued. 'Drinking cider and smoking fags in the local park. For the first time in my whole life, I had a sense of belonging. Other teenagers were interested in me, and I shut myself off from my mum and the rest my family.'

'Trust me,' I said. 'I know exactly what you mean.'

'Really?' She looked up, surprised.

'When I was a kid, I was a square peg in a round hole,' I told her, thinking back to my own troubled teenage years. 'I hated school and never fitted in with the "in-crowd". I only really had one friend, and things were not much better at home. I spent a lot of my time alone.'

Memories of my pal, Penny, and John from the travelling funfair came flooding back. The bright lights and loud music, the smells and the electric atmosphere of it all, filled my head as I told Tina about my own life on the road.

'The idea that you could move around and not stay in one place for very long really appealed to me, and before long, I started running away and sleeping rough. I got attached to a travelling fair and became friends with them all. I followed them all over the south-east, and sometimes went missing for days on end. The police got to know me by name, I ran away so often. They used to take me back to a social services safe house until my mum came and picked me up.'

'Nooo!' she piped up, her eyebrows raised in astonishment. 'You, having your collar felt by the law? You are kidding me, Michelle. You are the most level-headed, down-to-earth woman I know. You're one of those people who always knows what to do in any situation. How on earth did you end up like that?'

'It's true.' I laughed. 'I was a right bloody tearaway!'

'Was it sleeping rough and moving around that inspired you to start Dogs on the Streets?' she asked.

'I don't know really.' I smiled. 'It could have something to do with it, I suppose. But it was certainly a lot to do with a little Staffie called Poppy. She made me realise that I not only had to help, but I had to take that help out onto the streets where the homeless people and their dogs can get to us.'

Cradling her mug of hot chocolate, Tina went on to tell me how she had spiralled out of control, fallen into a seedy world of hard drugs and drifted aimlessly around, with nobody looking out for her, completely without direction, and with no support whatsoever. She then found herself in a relationship with a man who beat her black and blue, abused her and treated her like a worthless piece of meat.

'Something inside me just sort of snapped,' she said, silently crying. 'I'd had a bellyful of people not listening to me, not believing me and treating me badly. Packing a few things into a rucksack, and throwing a lead on Steve, I crept out of the back door early one morning and disappeared. Just Steve and me. I hitched by the side of the road, travelled all over the country without a care in the world. Eventually, we arrived in London, and, well, you sort of know the rest, Michelle.'

Her story was heartbreaking and infuriating in equal measure. I'd listened to so many tales just like Tina's, but it was no less of a privilege that she, like others before her, felt she could trust me enough to share her history with me.

Despite everything that later happened with her attack on me, I didn't feel that pressing charges against Tina was the right thing to do to. She was hurting, deeply wounded and damaged. She had lost control for a single moment, tied to a short fuse. She was struggling, confused and lost in a bad place, but had reached out to get help for her dog. She had become frustrated because the 'official' appointment time she had held to had been pushed back. This was nobody's fault, but disciplining herself to turn up at a time she expected to be seen was quite an achievement, and what happened must have felt like just another disrespectful disappointment. Despite her outburst that day, I knew at heart who she was, and what had happened to her in her past, and I had nothing but empathy for her.

Tina later apologised and luckily continued engaging with us. Deciding not to press charges for her assault on me was absolutely the right thing to do. Any other action would have lost her the only connections she had left: Dogs on the Streets and her own, wonderfully loyal companion, Steve.

CHAPTER 13

East to West

Arthur was rattling – I could see it straight away. His pyjama top was dripping with sweat, he was agitated, clearly stressed out, and rubbing his face vigorously. Withdrawal from class-A drugs is something I have witnessed a thousand times before. So many of my clients go through this. Many street people have long-term heroin habits and are signed up to methadone programmes. In recent years, Spice has become the chief drug of choice. It is literally everywhere, and is known by many names, including K2, Blaze, RedX Dawn, Paradise, Demon, Black Magic, Spike, Mr Nice Guy, Ninja, Zohai, Dream, Genie, Sence, Smoke, Skunk, Serenity, Yucatan, Fire and Crazy Clown. Its dramatic and disturbing effects can be seen each and every day in those corners of all our major cities where the destitute and the lost seem to congregate. People losing control of their own bodies, staggering through the streets with their arms waving and legs looking as though they have turned to jelly, have become an all too familiar sight. Their bizarre behaviour is captured on mobile phones by giggling teenagers, who then upload their booty as comedy items on YouTube and social media. The reality is anything but comical.

Most people get through their days with the help of a daily fix or some sort of pick-me-up, whether it be coffee, cigarettes or a regular dose of soap operas; personally, I live off chocolate cake! But most street people need drugs just to get them through the day. Out on the streets, whatever they need is readily available, and the temptation of a release from their emotional pain is far too much for most to resist. Counter-measures are in place, but they often feel like little more than a sticking plaster placed over a festering, open wound. Methadone programmes are now widespread, and Westminster City Council in particular seem quite forward-thinking in their approach. They have recognised that robust and well-funded addiction programmes can help bring down crime rates. It stands to reason that if you take away the overwhelming need for desperate people to get money for drugs by supplying them with clinically managed heroin substitutes like methadone and Subutex, then the levels of theft, antisocial behaviour and crime will inevitably go down. Investment by Westminster in strategies to reduce dependency on heroin has proved successful. Of course, it was not necessarily the well-being of street people that was the council's primary concern. The priority was rather to ensure the safety and welfare of local residents and the millions of visitors who flock to the area's tourist attractions. With their actions, the council was also protecting the income of the world-famous rate-paying shops and boutiques that Westminster is home to. The rationale informing the introduction of these initiatives mattered less to me and our team of dedicated volunteers than the outcomes however, which were only too evident. Whatever the motivation, my clients were benefitting.

However, the added complication that really can, and often does, throw a spanner in the works is the ever-present, much-dreaded but oh so popular Spice. The cheaper street versions are made in backstreet labs in dingy parts of town, and no two batches are ever the same. I'm reliably informed that the ruthless gangs who make this poison use ingredients like fish tranquillisers, scouring powder and even brake fluid. Anyone travelling through London will see Spice almost proudly displayed in the windows of so-called head shops all over Soho and in outlets up and down high streets, in places such as Camden in North London. Sold as legal highs, the brightly coloured packets with exotic names look just like little bags of sweets, and lay claim to outlandish health benefits while also stating 'NOT FOR HUMAN CONSUMPTION'.

There have been many occasions when we have had to deal with clients fitting and falling into unconscious slumps through taking this muck. We are advised to use orange juice and high doses of vitamin C to counter the terrible side effects. Drug and substance-abuse outreach workers have trained us how to recognise and react to different types of drug overdoses. I carry a defibrillator, as well as nasal sprays for use in the event of a heroin overdose (after calling the emergency services). The effects of drug withdrawal are very familiar to me, and I could see them in Arthur now. Up until this point, he hadn't displayed any withdrawal symptoms, but now, after weeks and weeks of seeming fine, it was clear Arthur had been secretly supplementing his habit. Now, he had fallen victim to the dreaded 'clucking' of withdrawal. I immediately took it up with the nurses.

'Has Arthur been given his methadone?' I asked at the nurse's station. 'He seems very unsettled.'

'I'm sorry,' the nurse said piously. 'I can't discuss patient care with you.'

'I am his next of kin, so it's allowed,' I told her, holding out the signed affidavit from Arthur appointing me as his spokesperson and advocate.

'OK,' she said, officiously peering over the top of her bifocals. 'Yes, it has been approved. However, his prescription has not come through, for some reason. I'm certain it's nothing more than an admin error and it will be sorted out as soon as possible.'

'But you do realise he has withdrawal symptoms?' I asked politely.

'Yes, we are more than accustomed to this, madam.' She smiled sarcastically. 'Bear with us; we have a lot of sick patients on this ward, and we will get there in the end.'

Marching back to Arthur's bed, I was furious. I knew that for the past few weeks he had been sneaking downstairs for a cigarette, and he had obviously also been taking delivery of street drugs to keep himself going until his methadone came through. But this really wasn't the way forward for him and he needed proper medical supervision and care.

'What's going on with you today, Arthur?' I asked him softly.

'I'm sorry, Michelle,' he whimpered. 'There is still no methadone, and I can't get anyone from outside to help.'

Arthur confessed that he had been using his mobile phone to get a message to a man he knew, and had been arranging to meet shadowy drug dealers at the back entrance of the hospital when he went out for a cigarette. However, he reached an impasse when his credit ran out, and he could no longer get anybody to deliver drugs to him.

'How long have you had a habit, Arthur?' I asked.

'I've been addicted to heroin for a long time, to be honest,' he sighed. 'I wish I could kick the habit. I've tried everything, but it's hard when you have been taking drugs for as long as I have. After a while, drugs become part of who you are.

'I lie in this bed, listening to all the bleeps and the machines, which seem to be making a noise around the clock in here. Being around so many seriously ill people all day makes my mind drift, and I think about myself in a way that I haven't for a long time. Life on the streets is about survival, and not living. In here, for the first time in a long time, somebody is looking after me, and I don't have to worry about what I am going to eat or where I am going to sleep; I don't have to think about keeping warm and clean or having access to a toilet. But more than this, lying in the bed makes me feel detached from the outside world. It's like I'm on hold, not part of the game, just a bystander watching from the touchline, completely out of it.

'Lithuania, my homeland, has been in my thoughts a lot lately. I think there is nothing quite like being homeless to make me think about home and what I have lost. You really don't know what you've got until it's gone. I had a wife and a child, a flat and a good job as an electrician. But then everything changed after the Soviets left Lithuania and independence happened. Our lives were transformed on that day – we were all so full of hope for a better future. The world felt like it was being turned upside down, and the whole of Vilnius was one giant party.

'We were all so happy to see the end of the misery and poverty that had been part of everyday life all through my childhood. My mother always had to queue for hours and hours just to get basic shopping and a loaf of bread, which was usually almost stale and hard by the time it reached the shops. We lived in an ugly concrete block surrounded by miles and miles of identical blocks, all filled with miserable faces. Yes, there were lots of good times when I was a little kid. In summer, we would go camping in the woods, swimming in the lakes, and we would build shelters and campfires to sit around and sing songs. It was a bit like your Boy Scouts. It was great fun. But to be honest, the Russians were never really any good at "fun".'

He gave a wry smile; the idea of Russians being 'fun' really seemed to tickle him. I sat and listened as he told me about his country and how things had changed with the end of the Cold War.

'We watched the Berlin Wall being pulled down by all those Germans and knew independence was on the way for us. There were protests on the streets and people formed huge human chains linking towns and cities as a sign of solidarity against the occupying Russians. Everybody was sick to death of them. They took all the best jobs, they moved all their own people into the best apartments in the cities to make sure there were more ethnic Russians than Lithuanians, who we called Litvaks, and they moved anybody they thought was undesirable to far-flung parts of the Soviet Union. The Federal Security Service and the Secret Police were constantly watching everything that anybody did or said. Looking back, it all sounds like some sort of crazy dream or a Hollywood movie, but it was real. It happened.

'By the time independence actually came in 1990, I had a wife, a little apartment and a job. But it was party time, and I openly admit I went a bit wild and off the rails. There was no more KGB and no more Russians with big boots and snarling Alsatian dogs ordering us around and telling us what we could and couldn't do. It was sex and drugs and rock 'n' roll, Western-European style, and I lapped up my new lifestyle and dived in headfirst.

'Over the next few years, I can see that I went too far, and there is always a price to pay for a living a life that I couldn't possibly afford. I fell in with the wrong crowd and started hanging out with very shadowy characters. By then, I had a baby son to support, but I was hardly ever home. I never saw him. Lithuania was flooded with drugs and the temptations of decadence. I drifted further and further apart from my family as I became more and more involved with crime and drugs. It was at this time that I started taking heroin.'

With his head in his hands, Arthur told me how his life had imploded; his family had turned their backs on him as he became caught up in a life of petty crime and gangland violence. The police were looking for him, and he went on the run, leaving his estranged wife and child to fend for themselves. With thousands of people leaving the country and others flooding back in after an enforced exile, Lithuania was plunged into economic crisis and chaos, and it was easy to disappear off the radar.

He wept as he poured his heart out to me. I was determined to remain non-judgemental as he told me how he begged, stole and shoplifted to survive as he hitch-hiked his way across Europe, looking for a new beginning somewhere else, over a thousand miles away from his home. Eventually, and almost inevitably, Arthur found his way onto the unforgiving streets of London.

Without a doubt, Arthur's was a dramatic tale, but one that required consideration of other cultures and an appreciation of the complications of being catapulted into a new world, light years away from the stifled freedoms and poverty of growing up in a totalitarian state. Arthur had drifted around the building sites of London and the south-east looking for cash-in-hand work as an electrician. But as his drug addiction got stronger and his mental health deteriorated, he struggled to cope with the pressures of life and ended up homeless.

'I thought about my family and friends in Lithuania all the time,' he said sadly. 'I still do; that place is so familiar to me, and I know every square inch of it. For many years, I never gave it any thought, but recently my mind has been drifting back to all those times, some good and some not so good, and I can just see myself walking through the streets of my childhood in the shadow of the massive Radio Tower that sits in the city centre and can be seen from practically everywhere you go. I tried to go home to see my family, but I was told that while I would have no problem getting into Lithuania, I would then struggle to get back into the United Kingdom. So, I never did get to go home.'

Reflecting on my many conversations with Arthur, I think this would be an appropriate moment to share some thoughts with you. As I explained earlier, all those who work with Dogs on the Streets lay themselves open to the knock-on abuse so frequently directed at the homeless, including accusations that our time and resources would be better directed towards more 'deserving' members of society. I have been accused of, at best, naivety, and, more pejoratively, of condoning drug-taking, drunkenness and the antisocial and/or criminal behaviour that sometimes accompanies dependency. Neither is true. I am only too aware of the social issues that arise from homelessness. Also, I am willing to say that the homeless individuals I meet are not always likeable. Some are manipulative, others lie, or are aggressive, or reveal attitudes I find offensive. I have learned, as with human interactions in any other setting, that first – or even second – impressions are unreliable guides to character or to my longer-term feelings about those I meet.

I always believe what the people I meet on the streets choose to share with me about their life histories. Although their tales are occasionally implausible-sounding, I under-stand only too well the multitude of disadvantages, accidents and inflicted cruelties, most of which are thankfully outside my personal experience, that shape pathways to rough sleeping. In many ways, it doesn't matter – I always start from where the person speaking to me is now. I am always interested in individual stories, but the true gift embedded in what somebody tells me is that I know it means they have the confidence to openly communicate with me; it shows that I am someone they have come to trust.

Whatever our own circumstances, when meeting new people, and even among those we have known for years, we generally try to portray ourselves in the best light possible. We hide the thoughts and deeds that we would rather others did not know, perhaps because we are concerned about being judged or regarded as less worthy of their friendship. How much greater must this fear be for those with nothing beyond their dogs and what they can carry?

However, I can only deal with situations as I find them. In relation to Arthur, there were occasional inconsistencies in what he told me, and over the time I knew him, he confessed to behaviour and activities that he felt shamed him, adding these to memories that became increasingly difficult for him to carry. Of course I listened. I never condoned, but neither did I ever judge. These things were irrelevant in terms of the man I had come to be fond of, and, more importantly, they were irrelevant to his right to dignity, proper care and compassion. It was these latter aspects that I could intervene to ensure. We all need to take people as we find them and strive to stand beyond the prejudices we all possess, in order to offer others one of the things we all value – acceptance.

Having taken the time to do a bit of reading to find out more about Arthur's home country, I learned that Lithuania declared the sovereignty of its territory on 18 May 1989, and declared independence from the Soviet Union on 11 March 1990 when it became the Republic of Lithuania. Huge changes swept the country, and the many freedoms that we all take for granted were given to the long-suffering people there. Of course, it wasn't a magic wand, and they faced massive hurdles and an uncertain future. Tragically, that uncertainty hit Arthur Dumbliauskas in a big way.

CHAPTER 14

Hackney Headache

'*Welcome to Hackney Council. Your call is important to us – one of our operators will be with you shortly.*' The pre-recorded telephone voice was robotic and humourless; it made me feel anything but important. Then another message drone chipped in, sounding even less interested: '*You are . . . number . . . thirty-seven in the queue.*'

It was Monday morning, it was raining and, to top it all, I'd woken up with a terrible headache. As ever, I had a thousand and one things to do, and my heart sank as I watched the usual deluge of overnight emails land in my inbox. For over a week, I had been battling to get through to somebody at Hackney Council, somebody with a modicum of common sense, somebody who could make a decision and get things done. Somebody who could help me to help Arthur and Kaizer find somewhere decent to live. However, navigating local government bureaucracy at Hackney Housing Department was proving to be more than a little tricky. Try as I might, I could never seem to get through to the person I needed to speak to, and I was passed from pillar to post. The elusive group of senior local government officers I was told I needed to speak to always seemed to be in a meeting, or away on leave, or tied up with some other, more pressing, matters. I had the distinct feeling that they would rather not have to deal with the complex issue of finding suitable housing for a homeless man on an end-of-life care plan, who also brought a dog with him. To them, Arthur Dumbliauskas was a bit more of a headache than they could be bothered with.

'You are . . . number . . . thirty in the queue.'

My ear ached and my already-banging head throbbed from the dreadful hold music, but I had at least moved up seven places in twenty minutes! Looking at the clock on the kitchen wall, I was beginning to get a bit fidgety, the usual anxiety based on my long and steadily growing to-do list. I knew the hospital were losing patience with Arthur and also with me, and a nagging worry was gnawing away at the back of my mind: where could he possibly go if they turned him out now? It was essential I made some headway in finding him somewhere to live.

'You are . . . number . . . twenty-two in the queue.'

Arthur had been in lying in that hospital bed for nearly three months, and he desperately needed to get out of there. It was my job to find somewhere fitting for him to live out his days as best he could. Kaizer also needed to be reunited with his dad, and time was running out. He'd been well looked after, fed and cared for, as well as exercised regularly. A spirited and lively young fella, he particularly loved the activities and stimulation play from our loving staff at the kennels. However, I could tell he was missing his dad, and it was getting to the time when he needed to get back to some semblance of normality, whatever that might turn out to be.

'You are . . . number . . . thirteen in the queue.'

The clock ticked, calls to me were going unanswered, and the messages and emails were continuing to stack up, but my resolve to help Arthur was undeterred. Earlier that week, I had spent an age and a day on hold for the Hackney Housing Department. When I had finally got through to a human voice, she asked me a series of questions that she was obviously ticking off from a checklist.

'Name?' she said.

'Arthur Dumbliauskas,' I answered.

'Are you the applicant?' she said.

'No, I'm his next of kin,' I said.

'Can you spell the name in full, please?' she said.

'A, r, t . . .' I recited slowly and clearly.

'Date of birth,' she said.

'16 October 1965,' I answered.

'Address?' she said.

'I am sorry, but he doesn't have an address – he's homeless,' I answered.

'I can't create a housing list profile without a current address,' she said.

'But he's homeless, so he doesn't have one.

'I can't put you on the list for housing without an address,' she repeated.

'But he's homeless,' I said again.

'All new applicants must provide an up-to-date address before they can be entered onto the system, madam,' she said.

'But he doesn't *have* one, he is homeless. That's why I am calling you. He has nowhere to live,' I begged.

'Madam, as previously stated, I can't add him to the list for housing without an address,' she said.

'But . . .' I stuttered.

'I am sorry, I need an address, madam,' she said.

'Oh, this is pointless.' I nearly slammed the phone down. This was hopeless – I was getting nowhere.

And now, a few days later, I had once again been hanging on the phone for over an hour, and I was losing the will to live! Of course, running a charity that regularly works alongside government agencies and social services, I was well used to red tape, paperwork and officialdom, but I have to say, the housing department at Hackney Council really was one of the more challenging agencies I have had to deal with. Admittedly, they were obviously under-resourced and under extreme pressure. That said, my priority was Arthur, and there was no way I was going to let him down.

Then, just as I thought I was getting somewhere, the line went dead. I was so outraged, I screamed out loud and kicked the kitchen bin! Slamming the phone down, I grabbed my coat and car keys and stormed out of the house.

CHAPTER 15

Hazardous Discharge

My battle with bureaucracy raged on, and my workload piled up higher and higher as a result of all the time I was spending at the hospital with Arthur, along with the hours spent trying to sort out a solution to his housing needs. My daily rounds of the streets of Soho and the West End were getting later and later in the day, and I was falling far behind. There was also a great deal of admin to do; I'd missed meetings and had a monumental pile of paperwork and bookkeeping to catch up on. All that was on top of looking after my own family! Already in a bad mood, I thundered, bag of supplies in hand, onto the ward. As I turned into Arthur's bay, my heart sank when I saw him sitting in the chair by the side of his bed, head in hands, crying.

'I don't what I am going to do, Michelle,' he sobbed. 'They are discharging me and asking me to leave.'

'They can't do that yet,' I fumed. 'You have got no home to go to. They can't just turf you out onto the street with nowhere go. I will see to it.'

'How can they expect me to manage a stoma bag, keep it clean?' he said. 'Some days, I struggle to walk in a straight line. My friend in Hackney, like me, had slept rough over many, many years. He was as tough as they come and so strong. But then he got ill, lost lots of weight and went really thin and sickly looking. One night we had bedded down in the old pub down from the station. He was fine; he had a bit of a chesty cough, but otherwise he seemed OK, given his circumstances. Then the next morning, I woke up and found him stone dead, still wrapped up in his sleeping blanket. He had died right next to me, and I didn't even notice. It was so tragic, so very, very sad. The police had to take him away, still in his sleeping bag. I never heard anything of him again; no funeral, no wake; nobody shedding tears, no nothing. He died alone and nameless. Nobody cared about him. I don't want to be found dead inside my sleeping blankets on the streets.

'Don't get me wrong, I want to leave, but where can I go like this? And how can I care for my Kaizer when I'm in this state?'

'Arthur, don't worry,' I said, putting my arm gently around him. 'You're leaving this hospital like this over my dead body.'

Knowing the hospital wanted him out, I had to have a plan, a strategy to carry into a meeting with the ward manager and admin staff. So keen was I to second-guess what their approach would be, I made hurried notes in my little book as I stormed onto the main corridor. Then, just as I made my way into the meeting, I had a brainwave, one of those lightbulb moments that pops into your head at the most unexpected of times.

'Mrs Clark, I'm afraid we have done all we can for Arthur,' the ward manager said, as we took our seats around a conference table in a side room, off the main corridor to a different ward. 'We can't accommodate Arthur any longer. He is well enough to be discharged, so we have no option but to do so.'

'You do realise Mr Dumbliauskas is homeless, don't you?' I asked, cueing up my trump card.

'Yes, of course,' she said. 'But this is a hospital and not a hostel. Beds are needed constantly.'

'But how are you expecting a vulnerable man in a fragile condition to manage a surgically installed stoma bag?' I asked, calmly and professionally.

'It is quite normal for stoma bags to be managed day to day by patients and members of the public,' she replied, looking directly at me.

'But without anywhere to live or anywhere to keep himself clean, Arthur will struggle to stop infections taking hold.' This was my opening salvo.

'We can teach him how to cope with this,' she said. 'We do have a great deal of experience, you know.'

'But you do realise that you may be in danger of breaching health and safety laws by being complicit in a threat to public health?' My broadside hit them full on. 'Do you realistically expect a terminally ill, homeless man with no meaningful end-of-life plan in place, living on the streets, to be able to properly dispose of used stoma bags? This is a potential biohazard advocated in no small part by you and this hospital.'

The ward manager looked across to her secretary. 'She may have a valid point,' the secretary whispered softly into her manager's ear.

'I'd like to read something to you all, directly from the Health and Safety Executive's website,' I said with a stony face, taking out my phone. "Management of healthcare waste is an essential part of ensuring that health and social care activities do not pose a risk of infection. To manage healthcare waste effectively, health and social care providers will need to consider: infection control and health and safety legislation; environment and waste legislation; and transport legislation."

That same day, the ward manager flipped her decision and agreed to allow Arthur to stay in hospital until I had found him and Kaizer somewhere appropriate to stay.

To me, it was a question of humanity; the very thought of turning a sick man like Arthur out on the streets with nowhere to go was abhorrent. While I fully appreciate that our NHS is overstretched and under-resourced, and that its staff are overworked as well as underpaid, it is essential for the good of society that we do everything we can to look after the most vulnerable, especially in the most desperate of situations. This is central to the ethos and concept of a national health service in the first place. Dealing with damaged personalities and vulnerable people is challenging, and a 'once-size-fits-all' approach can never work, as no two clients or patients are the same. This applies across the board, including to Dogs on the Streets and all the other agencies, health-care providers and charities that provide support for the homeless community.

The streets fill up with newly arrived homeless people faster than we can help and rehouse them. I never know what type of situation I could be walking into, and the vast array of stories and personal histories can be mind-boggling as well as heartbreaking. Any single factor in a list of horribly destructive, often connected, sources of trauma – domestic violence-related issues, sexual abuse, child sexual exploitation, trafficking, prostitution, drug addiction and alcoholism – can bring children, youths and adults onto the streets. These individuals are usually deeply and sometimes irrevocably damaged, often through no fault of their own, and it is vital that we do our best to care for them all. Working in environments such as this really makes me appreciate the love of my family and friends, as well as everything that I have and how fortunate I am. It also gives me perspective on my own considerable trauma. It really is a case of 'there but for the grace of God, go I'.

Arthur looked incredibly frail as I returned to his bedside to give him the news that he no longer had to worry about being discharged. He was hunched over his bed, clearly struggling to manage the pain in his tummy, but he still offered one of his trademark warm smiles, wincing through the pain.

'It comes on in waves,' he said, as he battled to straighten himself. 'I'm fine most of the time, and then all of a sudden it feels like a red-hot knife is plunging through my body. How did it go with the meeting?' he asked.

'It went well, Arthur,' I reassured him. 'It went very well indeed. And you aren't being discharged. Well, not yet, anyway. We need to concentrate on getting you back on your feet, reunited with Kaizer and in your own home, safe and warm, and with the right support in place to help you.'

'Thank you, Michelle,' he said softly. 'You truly are my guardian angel. I do not know what I would have done without you.'

'It's no trouble, Arthur.' I smiled as I packed his new Primark paisley-patterned pyjamas and a bottle of Lucozade into his bedside cupboard.

The more I learned about him, the more I admired his spirit and natural cheer. Street people try very hard not to present as nervous or hesitant, as this can be seen as a sign of weakness, leaving them open to attack or exploitation. It really is a jungle out there, and they need to keep their wits about them in order to survive. The tried-and-tested, sharp-witted adage that if you walk down a street as if you own it, you'll be safe, but if you look lost and unsure, you will be anything but, rang very true with Arthur. On top of that, though, he had an innate, big-hearted openness about him, and a trusting nature that was rare in its authenticity and warmth.

CHAPTER 16

Light at the East End of the Tunnel

'Hello there, may I please speak to Michelle Clark?' a soft-sounding voice asked ever so politely.

Bustling my way through the crowds of shoppers near Covent Garden, my outsized bags of essential supplies thrown over my shoulder and my trusty backpack, which was almost as big as me, nearly tipping me backwards, I'd somehow managed to grab my phone from the back pocket of my jeans.

'This is Michelle,' I replied, desperately trying to keep myself upright.

'Oh, hi Michelle,' he said. 'This is Kwasi from Hackney Housing Department. Is it a convenient time to talk just now?'

I suppose the sensible option would have been to gather my thoughts and call him back, to give me time to get in the right headspace, and also to dig out my notes with all the names and the dates of the multitude of posts and pillars through which I had passed. But now that they had finally called me, I did not want to miss the opportunity.

'I've been asked to give you a call about your family member, Arthur Dumbliauskas,' he continued.

'OK, that's great, thanks,' I said. 'I'm Arthur's appointed next of kin – he has no family. Are you familiar with his case? I have spoken to so many different people at the council over the past couple of weeks.'

'Yes, I think so,' he said. 'I have his case file here. Is this correct that he is homeless or currently has no fixed abode?'

'It is, yes,' I said, fearful of what he was going to say about the issues of needing an address in order to *get* an address. 'He's in hospital at the moment, but really he doesn't need to be there any longer. They have done everything they can possibly do for him. His condition is terminal, and he is not expected to survive any longer than six months. He has pancreatic cancer and a stoma bag fitted, so he will need to be somewhere clean and relatively near the hospital.'

'OK, I get the picture; he certainly is a tricky proposition for me,' Kwasi said gently. 'But nothing I haven't come across before. I promise you I will pull out all the stops and do my level best to find somewhere for him. Arthur is obviously in need of urgent accommodation, and given his added needs, we have to carefully consider where we locate him. Are there any more issues that I will need to know about in order to find a good match?'

'Well, he is a registered heroin addict,' I said tentatively.

I knew Kwasi would not be fazed by this. Addiction issues are so rife, and I was sure Kwasi would be accustomed to handling complex housing needs. Hackney as an area was not without its challenges. It was the issue of Kaizer that I was anxious about bringing up at this stage, but I knew I had to; there was no point in hiding the fact. There are very few hostels, private landlords or charitable housing organisations that will accept dogs. They claim they cause mess, noise and antisocial behaviour. Of course, they don't at all. But it just takes one person to complain about a dog, and the owner is out on their backside.

It is so difficult trying to convince people who simply do not understand what street dogs bring to their owners. Nor do they know that these animals almost always have impeccable conduct, never lose their tempers and invariably stay as close as possible to their owners. While recognising the almost-universal bias against letting accommodation to applicants with pets, I had nevertheless made Arthur a heartfelt promise that he would live out his days with his best friend, and I was determined make good on that. Every previous call I'd made to the council had turned adversarial, but I could sense an innate kindness and humanity in Kwasi. He was a man clearly dedicated to his job and willing to try his best to help.

160

'There is one other thing worth mentioning, Kwasi,' I almost whispered down the phone. 'Arthur has a dog, Kaizer, that he can't be separated from.'

The phone went ominously quiet.

'Er, right,' Kwasi said, eventually. 'So, what we are looking at here is finding decent-quality, safe accommodation for a terminally ill man on an end-of-life care plan, within reasonable travelling distance of his medical appointments, who is a registered heroin addict, and who also has a street dog that he can't be separated from?'

'Er,' I said. 'Yes, I'm afraid so.'

'Oh my days! Michelle, you're not asking much, are you?' Kwasi laughed. 'Luckily for you and Arthur, I do like a challenge. I will make this a priority today. Leave it with me, and I will update you as soon as possible.'

'Oh, thank you so much, Kwasi.' I smiled. 'It's great to know someone cares.'

I always believe that a sense of humour and a down-to-earth approach can move mountains. Arthur was caught up in the age-old, catch-22 problem that was the most common source of all the difficulties associated with finding decent accommodation for my clients. Over the previous few weeks, I'd had to stamp my feet and demand to be heard. The negotiations were very fraught and had caused a great deal of frustration. Arthur's set of circumstances and housing needs were not something that the council seemed equipped to deal with. There was no clear strategy in place, and they literally had no idea what to do with him. But eventually, push came to shove, and with the help of my 'new best friend', Kwasi, we finally appeared to be getting somewhere.

Racing through my day, all I could think of was getting back to the hospital so I could tell Arthur that there was light at the end of the tunnel. My faith in bureaucracy had been dashed so many times before, and over the years, I had become hardened to the disappointments, setbacks and stone walls that I regularly ran into when dealing with accommodation issues. Now, though, I did feel that some of the new housing officer's positivity had rubbed off on me. It was a refreshing change.

Autumn was setting in and the change in the air was tangible; I made a mental note to stock up on more socks! Racing back to my little car, parked up on double yellow lines near Charing Cross, I threw my empty bags into the boot and set off for the hospital, but before I'd driven out of the West End, Kwasi called with an update.

'I have some good news for you, Michelle.' I could almost hear his joy. 'I have managed to find a place that may well be a good fit for Arthur's needs!'

'Oh, that is good news.' I beamed. 'And will they accept his dog?'

'Yes, absolutely,' he replied confidently. 'I have been explicit with them about the special relationship he has with Kaizer.'

'Thank you ever so much,' I said, still smiling. 'He will be thrilled. He can finally get out of hospital and start living again. This means so much to us, Kwasi. I don't know how to thank you.'

'No thanks needed, Michelle,' he said. 'All in a day's work. I will text you the address straight away. The hostel manager is expecting your call, and he will hand over the keys and fill in the paperwork. Please let me know if you have any further problems. Good luck.'

CHAPTER 17

A Place to Call Home

'Now, take it nice and steady, Arthur,' I said, holding him up as he made his way down the stairs to his new flat. 'You can do it. You'll be OK.'

True to his word, Kwasi and the housing department moved fast to get Arthur out of hospital and into his new studio flat. The relief on Arthur's face as we packed up his things was tangible. However, as we snaked our way through the busy streets of East London, I grew more and more anxious as my sat nav took us further and further out of the area and away from everything and everyone he knew. Eventually, we pulled up at the hostel, which was at the far reaches of Hackney, bordering Haringey. Though the location was not ideal, I had to admit the building looked nice, and the area seemed relatively quiet and away from all the hustle and bustle of central Hackney. The hostel was spotlessly clean and orderly, and the manager seemed friendly and accommodating.

The hostel appeared to have previously been an old hotel, which the council had renovated into bedsits and studio apartments. Arthur's room was in the building's basement. It had one main spacious room with a little kitchen in a partitioned area and a separate bathroom. It was furnished with a bed, a two-seater sofa, an armchair and a little table to eat at. Even though the bedsit was below ground level, it was clean and well ventilated. Despite this, I could see that Arthur was going to struggle to get up and down the stairs as his condition inevitably worsened. I was also concerned that he was quite a few miles from the medical centre, the hospital and the chemist that he used for his medications.

'Oh, this looks nice, Arthur,' I said, pushing my nagging doubts to the back of my mind. 'What d'you think?'

'Oh my word, Michelle,' he said, clearly moved, as he sat down on his bed. 'This is the first real bed I have had of my own for as long as I can remember. Finally, I have a place to call my own.'

Putting a comforting arm around him, I sat down on the bed next to him. I felt like crying myself. It had been an emotional journey, filled with tears and uphill battles, yet something told me there was still more to come.

'Unpack and make yourself at home,' I told him. 'I'll go out to get a few things from the supermarket. I will be back as soon as I can.'

'Yeah, for sure.' Arthur smiled. 'I might even put my feet up and watch my TV!'

Dashing over to the local supermarket, I quickly filled a trolley with supplies. Arthur had nothing in, so I bought food, dog food, cleaning materials, washing powder and washing-up liquid. Making sure he had everything he needed, I packed it all into my car and headed back.

'None of this would have happened without you, Michelle,' Arthur said, as I bundled in weighed down with shopping bags. 'I have no idea how I can ever thank you.'

'Well, you can thank me, and the rest of Dogs on the Streets, by enjoying your time here, because this is what it's all about.'

With a peck on the cheek and gentle hug, I left Arthur alone to get acquainted with his new home; we needed him to be settled before we could think about reuniting him with Kaizer. I was so relieved to finally have found a home for him, but I couldn't help thinking that the stairs in the new place were going to prove to be a problem, and I also worried about how far away Arthur was from the hospital, the chemist and his friends. With his friends in mind, I thought it a good time to update a few of them.

'Hi, may I speak to Helen?' I asked, calling the lady who lived opposite the station, who had helped Arthur on that fateful night in June.

'Hi Michelle,' she answered. 'I saved your number, so I knew it was you who was calling. How are you? How are Arthur and Kaizer?'

'They're really good, Helen,' I said. 'Today has been a good day, for a change. Arthur told me that you and

Tom had been to visit him in hospital. That is so kind of you. I know he was thrilled to see you both, so I thought I would ring with an update and let you know how they are both getting on.'

'Yes, we were so worried about him that night,' she said. 'I couldn't sleep for worrying about him. I knew Kaizer would be safe in your capable hands, but I was desperate for news of Arthur. We were so upset when we heard about his diagnosis. I think about him every day, especially when I pass the spot where he used to sell the *Big Issue* outside the station. It's heartbreaking.'

'Well, you'll be very pleased to hear that things are now looking up for Arthur and Kaizer.' I heard Helen gasp joyfully. 'Please don't get me wrong, I didn't mean his cancer; Arthur's condition is never going to get better, we know that, but we have at least managed to find him somewhere decent to live, and I am now trying my level best to get him reunited with Kaizer.'

'Oh, that's wonderful news, Michelle,' she said enthusiastically. 'Tom will be thrilled too; I can't wait to tell him when he gets home from work. Arthur did say that it's exceedingly difficult to get accommodation for homeless people when they have dogs. But knowing him, he would rather sleep out on the streets, even with a terminal illness, than be forced to give up Kaizer.'

'Yes, this is very true,' I said. 'When the hospital first started talking about finding Arthur a hostel place themselves, he refused, because they wouldn't take Kaizer. He was even insisting on going back out on the streets with Kaizer so they could be together. He would do anything for his dog.'

As I spoke to Helen, the nagging doubts at the back of my mind that were telling me the saga was far from over started to resurface. Sometimes it can take the act of verbalising something to give yourself a little perspective, and then you realise it is a real-world problem. It was as if Helen became a sounding board for my fears.

'It sounds great,' she said to me as described his new flat.

'Hmm, yes, it does seem that way on the face of it,' I told her. 'But as we drove over there earlier today, it did occur to me that he was a long way away from his normal stomping ground.'

'And would that cause a problem, do you think?' she asked.

'I mean, it's great that he is out of hospital and on his way to being reunited with Kaizer,' I said, 'but those stairs are very steep. He can just about manage them for now, but I can't help worrying how it is going to be as he gets weaker and weaker. He's also a long way away from his doctor's surgery and the hospital, as well as the chemist where he needs to collect all his meds. He'd have to get a couple of buses every day.'

'But surely he could change GP and go to another chemist?' she said.

'Well, yes, he could, but the more I think about it, I'm not too sure, to be honest, Helen. Certainly, it's not a good idea to change his GP at this stage; he is in a routine, and they know him there now. He has complex needs, and he can struggle to look after himself properly. His stoma bag needs care and attention. The bags are delicate things that can explode, causing all sorts of risks of infection, not to mention embarrassment. I mean, can you imagine him being on a bus or a tube and his bag exploding? He'd go to absolute pieces. I'm sure you're right, though. He will be OK. I'm just being my old moaning self!'

'Oh no, Michelle,' she said. 'You've done amazingly well. I admire Dogs on the Streets immensely, and you are a modern-day superwoman!'

'Ha ha, I dunno about that.' I laughed. 'You're very kind.'

Putting the phone down after speaking to Helen, I couldn't stop myself. The worry and the anxiety started growing. It occurred to me that Arthur didn't know a living soul in the area; it was miles away, up near Finsbury Park, more North London than the East End, and light years from all his street friends and any familiar faces. However, my biggest worry was about how he was going to get around for his appointments.

CHAPTER 18

Autumn Fall

Within a week of Arthur moving in, my worst fears were realised when I got a call from the manager to say that Arthur had had a fall while coming down the stairs. By the time I got there, he was OK. He just had a few bumps and bruises, and was more than a little embarrassed, but otherwise he was as right as rain. All the same, his new home was proving to be even more of a headache than I had first anticipated. Speaking to Helen about his stoma bag bursting on public transport had really started playing on my mind, so I insisted on sending taxis to ferry Arthur back and forth to the centre of Hackney, something that was costing the charity a small fortune. This was obviously putting financial pressure on us, but equally I wasn't going to be responsible for preventing Arthur from getting the proper care he needed.

Through no fault of his own, Arthur found himself having to make regular trips to the hospital to collect his stoma bags, and would then struggle back home with the host of medical supplies that went with them. He also needed to make regular trips to his doctor, and daily trips to his chemist for his methadone. It was just too far for him to travel on public transport. I learned that what I'd hoped was an unfounded fear that an accident might happen with his stoma bag was actually a very real risk. At times, stoma bags can come loose, and do have the potential to explode. Arthur was also in a lot of pain, and all the cabs that I paid for to make life easier for him soon became an absolute necessity. To get all the services he had become dependent on – the doctors, the hospital, the medical centre – transferred to a different location was neither practical nor ethical.

Though I did manage to get his daily prescription of methadone moved to a more local chemist, Arthur was becoming increasingly stressed and upset; the move away from Hackney had meant the loss of all meaningful support, both medically and socially. Unsurprisingly, he started missing the support and kinship of all his street friends from within the homeless community. Ultimately, though, it was the struggle with the stairs that brought things to a head. Over the course of the next few weeks, the first fall I had responded to was followed by others, and attempts to leave his flat became more and more dangerous. In the face of his increased vulnerability, I brought in occupational therapists and social workers to report on his situation. They found that the accommodation was just not suitable for somebody who was very weak and in pain, and he could no longer go up and down steep stairs every day. Arthur had become a high risk.

'Right!' I could hear my familiar battle cries come out as soon as I opened my mouth. 'We'll have to find somewhere better, safer and closer to Hackney.'

'It's fine here, Michelle,' he said. 'I love my bed and my little flat. It is nothing. I will get used to the stairs. But I do miss my dog, I have to admit.'

'But Arthur, you have to face facts,' I told him. 'You're not going to get stronger; you are going to become weaker, and you are also going to need better support within easy reach of the people who can provide it. Leave it with me, I will sort it out,' I told him. 'I've got an idea.'

So I resumed my battle with the council. It had, in my view, become clear that Arthur needed vital support, not only as a rough-sleeper with an addiction but as somebody on an end-of-life care plan who could not independently look after himself or the needs of his dog. Framing this conclusion as a strong basis for my argument, I asked that Arthur be referred to a homeless hostel.

The following day, I contacted the homeless charity, St Mungo's. Their website said:

'At St Mungo's, we continue to work harder than ever to end homelessness and rough sleeping and change lives for the better. Year on year, we seek to provide solutions with, and for, people who are sleeping rough or facing homelessness, putting them at the heart of what we do to help them fulfil their hopes and ambitions.

We work with people to understand their goals and help them to achieve them in the best way to support them to rebuild their lives.'

St Mungo's is a brilliant organisation with a wide range of experience and a lot of dedicated staff. They pride themselves on taking a flexible approach and tailoring what they offer to the individual needs of rough-sleepers. Arthur certainly had individual needs that required tailoring.

However, the application for help made to them was rejected on the basis that they did not feel they could adequately facilitate his end-of-life treatment while also accommodating his dog, and this is obviously what I was pushing for. Arthur needed to be placed somewhere where he could get proper palliative care while retaining the companionship of Kaizer, who brought him great comfort, love, and a reason to get up and going in the morning.

My next step was to appeal St Mungo's rejection as being wholly unacceptable, arguing that they were discriminating against a man who had a terminal illness. By their own admission, he would have been considered for hostel accommodation had he not been so ill. But the fact was, Arthur had a medical support team and a Macmillan Nurse in attendance, and it was these people who would be shouldering most of the responsibility. I pointed out that as long as the correct protocols and procedures were put in place, all Mungo's had to provide was safe accommodation and observation. Arthur just needed back-up so that if he did become unwell, or collapsed, or anything untoward happened to him, there would be somebody on site who would alert other agencies and his health-care providers. Placing him in independent housing would leave Arthur isolated, vulnerable and without the essential, albeit minimal, level of protection I believed that St Mungo's could provide. I also offered assurance that myself and Dogs on the Streets would immediately step in to accept full responsibility for Kaizer and any of his subsequent care needs if something was to happen to Arthur.

Eventually, after a lot of hastily arranged meetings, a few raised voices and me stamping my feet like an angry school-girl, Arthur was offered a space in the hostel at St Mungo's in Hackney. Joy at this outcome very quickly turned to dismay, however, when Arthur at last received a formal offer from them. They had given him accommodation on the top floor, with the proviso that before he could move in, he had to prove that, in the event of a fire at the hostel, he could get down three flights of stairs in less than one minute.

'How the bloody hell are you going to do that?' I bellowed, as Arthur passed me the letter to read. 'This is ridiculous!'

'They say it is for health and safety reasons,' said Arthur despondently. 'Because I won't be able to use the lift in a fire. I can't move in until I pass this test. But I could never do that when I am like this.'

The application and the appeal process had taken me three or four weeks, and during that time, Arthur had deteriorated rapidly in front of my very eyes. Back at The Sanctuary, Kaizer had become very passive, as if on some level he knew things weren't right with his dad, even though they were still apart.

'Listen, Arthur,' I said, drawing him in conspiratorially. 'I'm sorry, but if you want to get out of this place, you are just going to have to do it. Go for it, Arthur, you can do this, and if you collapse at the bottom of the stairs, so be it. We can deal with that afterwards. But if you don't do this, you will not get into that hostel room, and we both know very well that it is perfect for you, except that it's on the top floor. It is exactly where you need to be right now.'

'Do you really think so, Michelle?' he asked, not sounding very confident. 'Do you really think I can do this? What if I can't? What if I fall? What if I lose my place in the Hackney hostel?'

'It will be fine, Arthur,' I said in my best motivational power tone. 'OK, it is a few flights of stairs, but they are very different stairs to this place. They are less steep, they're wider, and they're well-kept and spotlessly clean. There is also CCTV on every floor, so if anything does happen, help will be on its way to you in no time at all.

'Just tell yourself you can do it and get it over and done with. Imagine you're in the school athletics team, and you are all fired up for gold! Take a look around at the rest of the field – you're going to go up against a load of people in there who are out of their heads on drugs and booze;

they're not going to get down the stairs in under a minute, no way on earth.'

The hostel really was the right place for Arthur; I knew it and he knew it. So, when the day came for him to go up against the clock, he put his best foot forward and threw himself into the task at hand.

'Did I ever tell you that I was in the Soviet Red Army?' he asked me as he took his mark at the top of the stairwell, right outside what was to be his room, the prize for his gargantuan physical effort.

'No, you didn't.' I laughed. 'Is that true? Were you fighting for the Russians?'

'Absolutely, it is true, Michelle.' He giggled. 'But there was no fighting! More playing cards and seeing out the year of our national service!'

'On your marks, get set . . . GO!' shouted the support worker at the bottom of the stairs.

My motivational talk seemed to do the trick, and Arthur went for it, hitting the bottom, according to the stopwatch, just a few seconds over the one-minute mark. Looking up at the support worker, Arthur punched the air when he was given the thumbs-up. He had done the very best he could, and even though he was slightly over the minute, he had clearly accepted the challenge and smashed it. In the face of such determination and effort, they could hardly say no, and they accepted him.

CHAPTER 19

Back to Hackney

From the very first day he moved in, there was a marked change in Arthur. Despite his deteriorating health, his days became easier and, in many ways, his life got better and better. It's amazing what a few friends and familiar faces can do to lift a person's spirits. Arthur was back on his own patch. But the crowning glory was the day I brought his special friend back home.

'Hello, my darling boy.' I beamed as I opened the door to Kaizer's kennel. 'I've got a massive surprise for you today, my lovely, so you had better be on your best behaviour.'

Bounding out like a coiled spring, he leaped up at me, showering me with love and licks. He was clearly thrilled, sensing that something different was on the cards for him today. Before setting off for the East End, and his new life, I grabbed a new doggie bed from our stores, and we made our way to the car. At long last, the time had finally come for this loveable bundle of fun to be reunited with his dad after months apart. I couldn't wait to see Arthur's face. As soon as I opened the car door, Kaizer practically pirouetted out into the street, buzzing with excitement and panting furiously. We crept up the stairs at the back of the building and gently tapped on Arthur's door.

'Shhh!' I said, bending down to Kaizer.

He sat obediently and looked at me with his big chocolatey eyes as I held my index finger to my face and gently stroked his head. And with a whimper, he obediently settled down. Through the door, I could hear Arthur snoring. He had obviously fallen asleep in his new bed! I tapped the door more loudly. Nothing. We waited. Then . . .

'WOOF!' As if taking control of the situation, Kaizer let out an ear-splitting bark.

'Ah, I know that voice!' Arthur shouted from inside the room. Kaizer! My boy!!' he shrieked as he flung open the door and Kaizer jumped all over him.

Falling back on the bed under the sheer weight of his beloved dog's exuberance, Arthur laughed and cried tears of joy as his best friend covered him with his trademark sloppy licks. As I carefully placed Kaizer's new doggie bed in its rightful place at the foot of Arthur's bed, I couldn't hold back, and I erupted into floods of tears. They were together at last.

'This is the most perfect day.' Arthur beamed, turning to me as Kaizer began sniffing out all four corners of the room and marking his new territory.

'You've both done so well to get this far, Arthur,' I said. 'Now you have got to concentrate on your health. There's plenty of food and doggie treats in your cupboards. Kaizer has a new collar and lead, as well as a Dogs on the Streets coat to keep him warm. Winter is on the way, you know. Also, we've had him microchipped, so if he ever wanders off, he won't get lost.'

St Mungo's had a palliative care coordinator called Niamh Brophy. Niamh really engaged with Arthur. She helped him manage his pain and made sure he had everything he needed. Though I spent less time with him now, I did call in every day to see him; we had grown so close to each other in such a short period of time, we felt like family.

'Hello you!' I beamed on one visit, as Kaizer jumped up. 'How are you today, Arthur?'

'We are both OK, thanks Michelle,' he smiled. But straight away I could tell he had something on his mind; I could read him like a book.

'You can tell me anything you want, you know,' I said. 'I will always be here for you – you know that, don't you?'

'Yes, of course,' he replied. 'It's my birthday coming up, and it's going to be my last one. This has made me think a lot about my family and Lithuania. I know there is nothing I can do, but I can't help thinking about home and all my cousins back there and of course, my son. I haven't seen or heard anything from them for many, many years. My son won't even know who I am.'

'Your son lives in this country, doesn't he?' I asked tentatively, an idea forming in my head.

'Yes, his name is Laurynas, but I have no idea where he is or what kind of life he leads. I really have no information about him at all.'

When was the last time you saw him?' I asked.

'A long time ago,' he replied. 'He came looking for me on the streets. We had something to eat, and he told me about the death of a relative, but it didn't end too well, and I haven't seen him or heard from him since that day.'

It was clear to see that Arthur's cancer was taking hold of him. It was a strange thing, because, although he was so ill, it was almost as if he had been given a new lease of life. Talking to him and helping him to open up was so much calmer and less tense these days, simply because he was so much more relaxed. I don't know whether this was because of the reality of facing his own death or because of the environment at St Mungo's. Perhaps it was a combination of the two.

Arthur told me that when he was a young man, he used to play the guitar and write songs. He'd loved martial arts and, for a long time, was fanatical about karate. Even though the room he occupied was a very simple and sparsely decorated space, with just a bed, a small table and a few other bits and pieces, the comfort and sense of belonging he had gained from living at the hostel had really bolstered him, and he felt more able to talk about his emotions and what was going on inside his world.

'So many bad things have happened to me in my life, Michelle,' he said, his eyes looking straight into mine. 'For most of it, I have been alone; even with friends around me, I have been by myself in the world. The sheer horror of being homeless has gripped me so hard, it felt like I was being strangled and there was nothing I could do to stop it. I had no idea what to do or who to turn to; there was nobody – just me and my dog, and nobody else.

'Some days, I would curl up inside my sleeping bag on the cold, hard floor and squeeze myself tight, tensing every muscle in my body, just hoping the terrible feelings would go away. Inside, I was consumed by an overwhelming sadness, and I was so desperately lost, yet there were hundreds or even thousands of people walking past me, oblivious, like I wasn't even there; I was invisible, completely unnoticed, and passed off as nothing more than another hopeless scrounger and drug addict.

'I used to wish my life away, wishing that I had never been born, or that it would all end and the horror would go away. Drugs numbed the pain for a short time, but the swirling emotions came flooding back with more intensity. Music was one of the few things that ever took me outside of the hopeless loop that my mind would get stuck in. Music is very important to me. Will you make sure I get the right music played at my funeral, Michelle?' he asked, thoughtfully.

'Of course I will, Arthur,' I said softly, taking his hand in mine. 'You tell me what you want, and I will make sure to get it done. I won't tell anybody, until the time comes. I promise.'

'Also, I want to be cremated, Michelle,' he said seriously. 'My favourite colour is green, so it would be nice if people wore green, and I want people not to buy flowers or cards; I want them to make a donation to Dogs on the Streets.

'My favourite songs are "Price Tag" by Jessie J, "Missing You" by Puff Daddy and "You've Got a Friend" by The Brand New Heavies. But my all-time favourite song is "Ride On" by AC/DC.'

I vowed to Arthur that I would take care of his funeral arrangements – it would be the last thing I could do for him, and I fully intended to keep my promises. As I left the hostel, I jotted down the name of his son. Arthur's birthday was coming up, and I was determined to make it a special one. A post I put out on Facebook about Arthur's birthday circulated, and almost straight away, cards and gifts started arriving for him. On his birthday, I made my way across to Hackney.

'Come on, slowcoach,' I said to Arthur as he stood before the mirror, combing through his tatty hair. 'We're going to nip over to the café for a spot of birthday dinner.'

'You're too kind, Michelle.' He smiled, throwing on his jacket as we stepped out of the door of the hostel. We walked arm in arm along the high street, stopping at a small restaurant a few hundred yards from the hostel. 'Let's just pop in here quickly,' I said coyly. 'It won't take a minute.'

A cacophony of noise erupted as soon as Arthur stepped inside. 'HAPPY BIRTHDAY TO YOU . . .' The packed eatery burst into song, and Arthur's face lit up with sheer joy. As the crowd of friends and well-wishers around him parted, Helen and her partner Tom stepped forward, holding a massive AC/DC-themed birthday cake, complete with indoor sparklers and topped with a fantastic model of Kaizer. Through social media, Arthur's story had spread far and wide, capturing imaginations and pulling at the heartstrings of people from all over the world. Cards and gifts flooded in from the USA and Australia, as well as from across the country. Members of the public, hospital and hostel staff, and all his street friends from the local area were there, singing, dancing and, of course, drinking! Then, as Arthur blew out his candles, a photographer from the *Daily Mirror* fired off his flashbulbs. The following day, Arthur's story was printed in the newspaper alongside his photograph, his joy only too evident in his bright gleaming smile. A very special moment, captured for all time.

CHAPTER 20

Back to Hospital

Christmas is a strange time of year for Dogs on the Streets, as it is for all the homeless charities. The problem arises when the streets become packed with shoppers, all of them with money to spend and keen to get into the spirit of it all, spreading some festive cheer in the form of handouts as they pass. The takings from street begging go through the roof, as shoppers dig deep into their pockets, and a lot of rough-sleepers find themselves with more money than they can reasonably cope with. Fewer of them interact with us. A lot just seem to go missing, only to resurface in January with horrendous withdrawal symptoms after building up huge habits fuelled by Christmas donations. Street robberies, fights and violent crime escalate as large numbers of the homeless community battle with mental health problems and addiction in the wake of the so-called party season.

This year, though, my thoughts were focused on Arthur Dumbliauskas, who by early December had taken a turn for the worse. He had to fight to get out of bed, struggled to eat anything, and never left his room. Skin and bone, his complexion pale and sickly, Arthur had lost a dramatic amount of weight and was becoming gravely ill. With Kaizer loyally curled up in a ball by the side of his bed, the room glistened with lights as I walked in, shopping and supplies in hand. We had decked out his room with Christmas decorations and twinkling fairy lights, after he had told me he particularly loved the Christmas lights in the West End, and this would be the first time he could remember that he had missed the big switch-on.

'Michelle, I need to ask you something,' he said feebly, clutching my arm as he lay in his bed. 'I need you to take Kaizer for me. I can't look after him any longer, and he needs more than I can give him.'

'Arthur, you don't have to worry about Kaizer,' I told him. 'We've already got a good home sorted out for him when the time comes. He'll be fine. But I really think it's time to get you back into hospital, my love. Don't you think?'

'Yes,' he answered weakly, his weary eyes heavy with sleep. 'I think you are right.'

As we waited for the ambulance to come, Arthur handed me his rucksack and his little black purse, containing his bus pass and a few other bits and pieces. 'Please look after these things for me, Michelle,' he whispered. 'Take them out from time to time and think of me.'

'I will, Arthur,' I said, kissing his forehead as the para-medics came in. 'I will take care of Kaizer, and I will make sure he's happy and well looked after. I'll come to the hospital as soon as I can.'

It was just two weeks before Christmas when Arthur was admitted back into Homerton. By the time I got to the hospital, Arthur was completely dazed and confused; I don't think he knew where he was or what he was doing. I watched him stagger to the toilet, insisting that he could do it by himself and that he didn't need a bed pan. Within seconds, I heard an almighty crash. Dashing into the cubicle, I found Arthur flat out on the floor, with a huge gash in his head. He had fallen over and smashed his head open on the toilet. His condition was now critical; there was nothing they could do for him except manage his pain.

I became increasingly concerned about him. It just seemed that his end-of-life care was not how it should be. He was having wild hallucinations that were terrifying him; he was thrashing about in the bed and appeared totally drugged up to the eyeballs. To me, he was in the wrong place, and I felt I had to get him out of there as soon as possible.

From his bedside, I called a hospice and told them his story, stressing the urgency of his situation. I practically begged them to take him – if nothing else, to spare his dignity. We then got the Macmillan nurses to call them directly, and luckily, on Christmas Eve, Arthur was trans-ferred to the wonderful St Joseph's Hospice in East London.

He was in a desperate state by the time we got him there, but the staff at St Joseph's went above and beyond the call of duty, and treated us both unbelievably well, almost like a married couple. They added so many little unsought and unexpected touches of kindness; it was heart-warming to witness such dedication and care. They really were all angels.

'I got you a little Christmas prezzie, Arthur,' I said, handing him a small, gift-wrapped box. 'It's not much, but I thought you could make good use of it.' His face lit up as he opened up the box and took out an MP3 player. 'You can listen to all that terrible AC/DC music now!' I laughed.

'Thank you, Michelle.' He smiled. 'I haven't had a chance to get you anything, I'm afraid.'

'Oh, don't be daft,' I said, putting the music player on charge for him. 'You lie back and listen to your music. I'll be right here, by your side.'

What he didn't know was that I'd arranged another very special present for him. I had finally found his son, Laurynas, and had contacted him. When Arthur had told me about the time his son had come searching for him on the streets of London, seeking him out to tell him about the death of a relative, he had mentioned that he and his son had attended the funeral together. This gave me a clue on where to begin my search. Remembering the deceased friend's name, I located the funeral director who had made the arrangements. They, in turn, passed on my details to another relative, an aunt of Arthur's. She called me and I explained who I was and why I was looking for Laurynas.

What I thought was terrible music really relaxed Arthur, and together with the expert pain management available at St Joseph's, he was calm and relaxed when I arrived on 27 December. I knew who was outside waiting to see him, but obviously Arthur had no idea.

'Arthur,' I said, gently tapping him on his shoulder. 'Turn off your headphones, there's some people here to see you.'

'Who is it, Michelle?' he asked, his voice sounding cracked and tired.

Silently smiling at him, I watched as Laurynas, his wife and their two little girls walked into the room. Stretching out his arms towards his son, Arthur's eyes welled up with tears.

'I'm going to leave you to catch up,' I said as father and son hugged, grabbing my bag and a few things, then getting up to leave.

Making myself scarce for the day, I had a walk through the streets and watched all the people out enjoying the festive period, laughing and joking as they hurried off to the sales in their new Christmas clothes. The contrasts in society never pass me by.

Later that night, after Laurynas had gone, I went back to spend a few hours with Arthur. Although he was exhausted and didn't wake up, I sat silently at his side, listening to his laboured breathing as he slept. I thought about the journey that had brought us both to this place, at this point in time. In the following days, I made as many visits as I could. Strangely, going back and forward to the hospice became something to look forward to and enjoy. The staff at St Joseph's were amazing, really lovely. Although Arthur was the patient and was made very, very comfortable, I felt that both of us were in the best of hands. They even brought a drinks trolley round and offered us whiskey, beer or a glass of wine!

'Are we allowed to drink in here?' I asked. 'I expected a cup of tea and maybe a biscuit!'

'You can have what you like, Michelle.' One of the nurses smiled and handed me a large glass of wine.

They knew I was a charity worker and not one of his relatives, although Arthur had appointed me his next of kin. Nevertheless, I was treated like a close relative. The humanity and compassion shown by everyone we came into contact with there was really outstanding.

With his breathing becoming increasingly laboured, it became clear that Arthur was very close to the end and in a lot of pain. He found it hard to find the energy reserves to even talk. When he did, he spoke about his son and new grand-daughters. Most of the time, we sat for hours in complete silence. Every now and then, though, he would motion for me to come closer and gently whisper things to me.

'I want to be cremated, Michelle,' he said, my ear just inches from his lips. 'And after, I want to stay with you. I love you, Michelle Clark. You are my angel. I love you.'

As he spoke, I felt a lump at the back of my throat. Sitting there holding hands with Arthur in his dying days made me examine my own life, confront my own mortality and question what good I had brought to the world. Through knowing Arthur, I realised that the cathartic journey that started with meeting Kenneth and his dog, Prince, and then continued with Poppy the Street Dog, leading me to work with homeless people and their dogs, was born out of a deep trauma that I had been carrying around all these years. Sometimes, I could feel the pain and the horror that he so often spoke about, as well as the unbearable weight of simply being alive, and my heart ached to feel loved, wanted and valued. But in all my days, I simply could not recall one of my clients telling me that they loved me in the way that Arthur Dumbliauskas did.

As he drifted back into sleep, I took off his headphones and tucked him securely into bed. It was late, the early hours of the morning, and I had to head off home. It was an icy-cold night, and the streets were almost empty. Staring into the orange glare of the streetlights as I drove through the East End and out into the darkness of North London, I felt a wave of emotion come over me. Reflecting on everything that had happened to me and thinking back to that teenage tearaway, sleeping rough and following the funfair, my memories turned to the little Staffie who came to visit me and say hello as I tried to sleep under the concrete stairwell of that dingy block of flats. I can't explain why she came back into my thoughts. In my mind, I felt it was some sort of reflection of Poppy, as if someone or something was sending me a message: you are loved and you are wanted.

There was an eerie silence as I locked up my car, my feet crunching on the stone gravel of the driveway. Opening my front door, I had a sense that Arthur must be nearing his time. I was awoken by a call at 3am, my phone lit up in the pitch black. It was a call from St Joseph's, and I instantly knew what it meant. They told me Arthur's breathing had become more and more shallow. They very kindly put the phone to his ear so I could speak to him, just in case I didn't make it back to the hospice in time. Throwing on some clothes, I dashed out into the freezing January night air and started my car. Racing through the streets of East London, a strange calm came over me; a tear trickled down my cheek, and I smiled at some of the memories we had built together. It somehow felt like the end of a long journey.

'Michelle,' a nurse said to me as I walked into St Joseph's, 'I'm really sorry to have to tell you, but Arthur has just passed away.'

CHAPTER 21

Goodbye, Arthur

Dozens of people packed into the small chapel at the City of London Crematorium, a peaceful and beautiful resting place and a Grade I-listed building, rich in history, architecture, nature and wildlife. Its beautifully tended, tree-lined avenues contrasted sharply with the concrete sprawl and urban crises that typify the East London streets Arthur had lived on. To me, it was a fitting setting for a true Londoner's memorial service.

Through the power of social media, Arthur's story had won the hearts of many members of the public. They had made the time to come and pay their last respects to a man who had once been an invisible shadow, curled up in a ball in a shop doorway or a run-down, abandoned old pub, but who came to embody the spirit of giving, through the love of his dog, Kaizer, and his brave battle against cancer.

At this point, Kaizer was still with me, but, with Arthur's approval, we had found him a suitable home with a couple who knew him, and who could undoubtedly look after his every need. It was hard for me to make the decision not to take Kaizer to his dad's funeral, but I felt his grief was just too deep. After only relatively recently being reunited with Arthur and then separated once more, I felt being there would only upset and confuse Kaizer at a time when he was already dealing with his own deep sense of loss. Although I understand people's criticism of me for not bringing Kaizer to the funeral, I still think it was the right decision.

The day before the funeral, my friend and I had gone to the flower market and bought several hundred roses that could be sponsored by supporters for £5 each. The money we raised went towards the funeral expenses, as well some reclining chairs to be used in the hospice. In accordance with Arthur's wishes, we offered the rest of the flowers for mourners to buy for a pound each. Money raised went to support the work of Dogs on the Streets. Staff from the hospital, St Mungo's and St Joseph's all turned up, along with some of Arthur's street friends, who had made the journey to see their pal off. Arthur's son, Laurynas, also attended, and sat near me at the front of the chapel. I was so happy that he could come; it would have meant the world to Arthur to have his son at his funeral. And there were so many familiar faces from different agencies and charities. Caseworkers and outreach staff, whom I work alongside but never really get to speak to, turned up in solidarity and support.

Almost everybody wore green, and those who didn't carried something green instead.

I couldn't hold back the tears as Arthur was carried in by pallbearers to the sound of one of his favourite songs, 'Price Tag' by Jessie J. Although Arthur was brought up in the Catholic tradition in Lithuania, he opted to have a secular celebrant conduct his service. Hannah Jackson-McCamley, whom I had met with to go through the eulogy, led a very touching celebration of Arthur's life and the impact he had made on everybody present. She was so caring and passionate in her address, beginning, 'Good morning and thank you for joining together today to honour the life of Arturas Dumbliauskas. Perhaps he was better known to you as Arthur; a friend, a father and compassionate owner of his beautiful dog, Kaizer.'

Hannah continued, 'It may be that many of you were introduced to Arthur through Kaizer's story, so entwined were their lives. It may be that many of you here didn't meet Arthur at all in his short life. But his story triggered something within all of you here, and many, many more people from across the UK and as far away as Australia, who have followed his tale and sent so many thoughtful condolences.

'Today's service will pay tribute to a man. Not a homeless man, nor a man whose life should be defined by the manner of his end or the circumstances he found himself in. Arthur was a human being with a life and a story, and irrespective of how one's life pans out, we each deserve to be recognised, ideally in life, but most certainly in our death. We all have the same beating heart, the same colour blood, we all come into the world the same way, and we all deserve to leave it with honour and respect. We must give thanks to Michelle Clark and the team at Dogs on the Streets for giving Arthur the respect and support he deserved over the last months of his life. It was through Michelle's dedication to her work helping dogs and their owners, who live on the streets, that Arthur's story came to light.

'Arthur was just fifty-three when he died on 11 January. Through his conversations with Michelle, and from what his son Laurynas has said, he had enjoyed happy times in his life, many in the last year, irrespective of his declining health. He did discuss his funeral, hence today being a cremation, the musical choices, the request for us to wear green, and the beautiful roses. He did not want today to be filled with gloom, but we cannot fail to mourn a life passed. Since finding himself homeless, Arthur only wanted respect and to be acknowledged as a person; not someone invisible on the street.

'We must ensure that today he is treated with the reverence he deserves. Arthur was based in Hackney Wick, where he sold the *Big Issue*. He was a well-known face and well regarded in the community. They always looked out for him. In April last year, his health took a turn for the worst. This is when locals Helen and Tom, who are here with us today, contacted Michelle from DOTS regarding Arthur's cherished dog, Kaizer.

'Arthur had been rushed to hospital and his playful, energetic, young dog needed a foster home. Michelle settled Kaizer in their emergency kennels and went to meet Arthur at Homerton Hospital. On meeting him, Michelle realised that this man had no support. He had been isolated from everyday life for so long, and he really needed someone. We could say anyone would do it, but we know that is not true. Michelle went above and beyond what most of us would do, even for those closest to us. But Arthur and Michelle became firm friends – she always had his back, and it meant the world to him to have her walk through his final ordeal with him.

'Arthur's later life had not been easy. But he had an enjoyed a happy childhood. Laurynas told us that his father was born in Lithuania in 1965. He was an adored and spoilt only child who wanted for nothing. As a young man, he had trained in martial arts and karate; he was very skilled and proficient. He spent a year in the Russian army, and was a well-trained, professional electrician. He worked hard. His love of music is well renowned, and we will hear some of his favourite songs throughout the service. But it may surprise many that during his married years, when his son was growing up, he loved to play the guitar and sing songs, especially songs he had written himself. He loved to share his music with his son and many others.

'Through circumstances and events unknown to us now, Arthur moved to the UK twenty years ago and lived on and off the streets for much of that time. London can be a tough place to live at the best of times. But living on the streets must have been unimaginably bleak. A life lived in such austerity and desolation would surely make one bitter, dejected and hateful. But Arthur, in large part thanks to his dog Kaizer, had reason to remain optimistic.

'I'm sure many of you are dog owners and can attest to the power an animal can have over you. I prefer to say animal companions to pet, and I believe the animals in our lives can have a truly healing effect. They can give you a reason for being, for facing each new day, irrespective of the harsh realities or the difficulty in circumstances.

'Dogs don't judge, they love and support unconditionally; they don't ignore you, they don't let you down. Czech author Milan Kundera said, "Dogs are our link to paradise. They don't know evil or jealousy or discontent."

'Kaizer gave Arthur what no human had offered in a long time. Kaizer kept Arthur going, and never more so than when he was diagnosed with pancreatic cancer in July. Through Michelle's relentless dedication to Arthur and her belief in the importance of animals to the homeless community, she fought to get Arthur secure accommodation with St Mungo's alongside his trusted companion, and also the palliative care team that would see him through his final months. Michelle would see Arthur daily, and he would light up when she was there. She recognised consistency was something Arthur hadn't experienced in a very long time, and this was what he needed.

'As Michelle posted on DOTS' social media channels, Arthur and Kaizer's story reverberated throughout the DOTS community and beyond. Keen to give him a final birthday party, Michelle asked that supporters send a birthday card to Arthur. He was overwhelmed by the response. The *Daily Mirror* covered the story, and he told them, "I got fifty-four cards, a lot from people I don't even know. Last year, I didn't get any." He was astounded yet overjoyed that people actually cared.

'He stayed at the hostel in Hackney with Kaizer for as long as possible, but Kaizer, not yet two years old, did become too much. As a Staffie-Ridgeback cross, Kaizer is strong and a little bit bonkers, and with so much energy. As Arthur started to ail, Kaizer was rehomed with Chris and Rita, who are here with us today; it was a relief to Arthur to know his beloved dog was in good hands. DOTS assured Arthur that Kaizer's support would continue when he was gone.

'As he moved into St Joseph's Hospice, Arthur was able to receive twenty-four-hour support. He had his own room, and was happiest listening to music, wearing his beloved AC/DC T-shirt. As a huge music fan with a vast and eclectic knowledge, Arthur was able to revel in his favourite tracks. For the first time in many years, Arthur felt safe. This may seem ironic, given the cancer he faced, but he could finally relax in the knowledge his few belongings wouldn't get stolen, that he wouldn't be sleeping out in all weathers; he was finally granted some security.

'"Yes, I think about death when I get pain," he said, "but for me now, I just think about the joy."

'He was finally getting some reprieve from the tumult of his life. He faced the cancer head-on, and took it all in his stride. Yes, he would get sad, but he appreciated what the final months of his life gave him . . . Michelle and the team worked hard to bring Arthur some sunshine. As well as the birthday party, Michelle and her trusted dog groomer Fiona gave Arthur a Prosecco night – a glass of wine, his favourite music. "This is the way to die," Arthur proclaimed.

'He had hoped to see the Christmas Lights in the West End, but Arthur's health had deteriorated by mid-winter. But that didn't stop Michelle bringing the lights to Arthur – decorating his room with bright lights to make him smile. He spoke so fondly of her, and she really did change his life, even if just for a short time. To quote Arthur himself, "She is an angel, my angel."

'Although Arthur had not seen his family for some time, he was overjoyed to be reunited with his son Laurynas and meet his son's wife and his grandchildren in December. On the slideshow behind me, you can see a picture of the family together. Arthur was so proud of his son and the family he had created. He had great hope for their futures.

It meant so much to Arthur that they were able to spend some time together, and he would be overjoyed that his son is here today.

'It may sound odd, but the last year of his life may have been amongst the happiest in a long time. He was at one with what lay ahead, and made peace with how his life had gone before. Arthur was overawed by the messages he received and delighted that he was finally being recognised as an equal to any other . . . not just a homeless man. He was no longer invisible or a face by the kerb, but was being treated, rightly so, as a human being.

'"I want a quick death," he said, "to be comfortable, without any pain. I know it's coming. But I know I'm not going to die on the street. I'm going to be with people who respect me and support me for who I am."

'Arthur was kind, caring and respectful, and finally he got some of that back, thanks to DOTS, St Joseph's and St Mungo's and the many, many supporters who backed him, far and wide.'

I kept my promise and had 'Missing You' by Puff Daddy, 'You've Got a Friend' by The Brand New Heavies and 'Ride On' by AC/DC played during the service. The closing song was 'Let It Be' by The Beatles.

It seems like an odd thing to say, but I really do feel that the last few months of Arthur's life *were* some of his happiest times. He was terminally ill with cancer, unable care for himself independently, and living in a homeless hostel while coping with a stoma bag. He had little or no possessions to call his own. What he did find in those last days, though, were the love and the connections that he thought had vanished from his life.

To have been touched by this beautifully warm, loving man was both a privilege and an honour. Love finds us in the most unusual times and places, and bites you playfully on the bum when you least expect it. Both Arthur and Poppy, in my mind at least, became bright, shining beacons of light in a murky world of poverty and destitution. The humanity and spirit they epitomised will be a part of Dogs on the Streets for many years to come.

Arthur's last ever words to me were: 'You are my angel, I love you, Michelle.'

I knew it was time for him to go, but inside I was thinking, 'Please don't leave me.'

RIP Arturas Dumbliauskas, 11 January 2019.
Forever in the soul of the work we do.

Voices From Clients of DOTS

'My dog Rosie is my pride and joy. I don't know what I would do without her, and am very grateful to have met Michelle and to have used her charity DOTS.'

Graham

'When things go wrong, DOTS are always ready, willing and able to help.'

James

'My dog's name is Diamond. She is simply the best, she gives me the strength to be a caring and responsible owner and person. She loves other dogs and people. They say a dog is for life, and never a truer saying. Diamond is my life.'

John

'I would be lost without my dog; she is my best friend and my family. But she wouldn't be here today if weren't for Michelle and DOTS.'

Andrew

'I found it very hard to access services as I was homeless on the street with my dog. If it hadn't been for DOTS, I feel we would both be very ill indeed. I actually feel blessed to have met Michelle.'

Princess Leia Organa

'Michelle, the team at DOTS and the vets who give their time for nothing should be given a medal.'

Allie

'Michelle taught me that there is always love. Without love, we have nothing.'

Colin

'My dog Nino means everything to me; he gets me through my darkest days and is a true friend.'

Danny

'London is a better place because of people like Michelle and DOTS.'

Graeme

'The dedication and love Michelle and the rest of the team show me is never-ending.'

Claire

'My dog Striker is happy and healthy thanks to the vets at DOTS. I cannot thank them enough.'

Andy

'DOTS gives me a sense of belonging. I will be forever grateful to Michelle and the team.'

Carl

'When people often ask me if would sell my dog, I always give the same answer: would you sell your child? I'd be lost without my girl, she is everything to me, the reason I get up in the morning, the reason I carry on, the reason I breathe. I'm so grateful for Michelle and DOTS.'

Jane

'It means everything to know there is someone out there who cares, and to know that if my girl is ever sick or I'm unwell and need help, there is someone there for us twenty-four hours, seven days a week.'

Amy

I have a dog named Honey who is now ten years old. She's my first-ever dog, and without her, I doubt I would get out of bed in the morning. I love my dog so much I can't really put it into words. This is my second time visiting DOTS – without this charity, lots of homeless dog owners would really find it hard to get treatment.'

D. Moffatt

'I have known Michelle for over ten years. She has helped me with food and vet treatment for Lola. I met Michelle when I was on the street, and although I am now living indoors, she still helps me with dog food, vet treatment and support. Michelle is brilliant.'

Gary

'I was made homeless before the pandemic; DOTS have been a godsend. I suffer from anxiety and mental illness and with my dog's joint issues, DOTS have been a real big help with his medication. It's been good to know that the help I get from DOTS is readily available.'

Chris

'When no one loves you, the dog loves you. My mum got sectioned recently and the dogs really helped me. They are like fur angels and you can take them anywhere, on trains and buses. DOTS have been amazing when I have had no money, they have always been there to support and listen. They don't just care about dogs, they care about people as well.'

Joseph

'Life without my dog, my baby, would be unbearable. She is my life and more. DOTS – Christ, where would we be without them? Our angels – our lifeline.'

Liam and Rosey

'I have been coming to DOTS for over four years. DOTS have been looking after me and Revel. The vet treatment is a godsend, and we are supported with dog food. If it wasn't for DOTS, Revel would probably be dead.'

David

'DOTS give a very good service – they feed the dogs, give them good medical help and try to help the owners as well. It helped me a hell of a lot. Thank you for that.'

Nelson

Acknowledgements

Special thanks to Joseph Cusack who supported me immensely putting this book together. Your dedication and support will always be with me.

Special thanks also to my publishing team at Orion for bringing two books to life and to everyone that helped bring this story together in memory of Arthur and Kaizer.